PRODGEY

The Penal Press

THE
PENAL
PRESS

Russell N. Baird

Northwestern University Press

Evanston 1967

*Russell N. Baird is Professor of Journalism
at Ohio University, Athens, Ohio.*

To William Keteltas,
wherever he may be . . . .

CONTENTS

PREFACE

ONE HOPE for an improved public understanding of correctional institutions rests with a little-known band of convict editors and the prison newspapers and magazines they produce: the penal press. This virtually forgotten branch of the fourth estate is trying to raise its collective voice so that news of the faults and needs of our prisons will be heard and heeded by the general public.

Americans have a remarkable ability to forget about the people they put into prison. The commission of crimes, the arrest, the trial, the confinement—all receive publicity. But the days, months, and years that the headline-makers spend behind bars roll on incessantly without public attention.

In spite of the millions of dollars they spend keeping criminals locked up, very few taxpayers ever bother to visit a penal institution to see how their money is spent. Riots, and sensational stories of violence, perversion, and administrative scandal occasionally raise a minimum of public attention for a brief time.

On the whole, however, our country's 220,000 prisoners exist in a forgotten society. This society, partly because of lack of public attention and financial support, breeds even more of the crime that prisons are expected to reduce.

Men who leave prison often commit other crimes and return to it; two out of three inmates of our prisons have been there before. The public must face the fact that, except for the few who die during their terms, all prisoners return to the free world. Whether they return as criminals or as productive citizens is determined, to a large degree, by our prisons. Aside from humanitarian reasons, a concern about the wise investment of public money should make an increased awareness of our penal system's shortcomings a matter of interest. Until the public develops an interest in prisons, and has a better understanding of what modern penology can do, very little progress can be made.

This book is the story of the penal press—its history, its goals, its problems, and its successes. Hopefully, it will draw merited attention to the penal press, and to the institutions the penal press is dedicated to improving.

Insofar as possible, this study has been restricted to the penal press, leaving out other aspects of correctional administration. The author makes no pretense of being an expert in penology; he is a journalist taking a look at an unusual segment of the American press.

To gather facts for this study, questionnaires were prepared and sent to all state and federal correctional institutions in the United States. Hundreds of penal publications were read, and selected ones were analyzed. Several penal institutions were visited for talks with editors, wardens, and the administrator who had responsibility for the publication. Old files at the Library of Congress and other libraries provided historical background. The interest and cooperation from all sources allowed a breadth of coverage that was not previously thought possible.

With material in hand, the problem then became one of how to tell the story of this interesting facet of journalism. It was decided to let the editors and administrators tell the story in their own words wherever possible. A point so often made by penal press writers is that only a convict can know what it is like to be in prison; thus, it seemed fitting that they tell their own story. There is, therefore, a heavy reliance on quotations from the convict editors and their supervisors. And rather than waste words on the hopeless task of describing the kinds of writing produced in prison, selected offerings are presented for the reader's own appraisal.

To avoid repetitive and unnecessary footnotes, the material taken from interviews and questionnaires is not specifically noted; all quotations and statistics are from these sources unless otherwise indicated. Also, detailed information that probably would not be of interest to casual readers has been confined to appendices where it may be found by anyone desiring the specifics.

In quoting from inmates' publications, every effort was made to insure that credit for authorship would go to the proper person, if such credit were desired. The possible need for anonymity on the part of convict writers was a matter of some concern; under no circumstances did I want to add undesired publicity to the burden of someone in confinement who, for personal reasons, wished to remain anonymous. The decision to use the authors' by-lines as originally published was made after interviews and correspondence with inmate editors revealed an insistence that they be fully credited for their work. Their view was that any editor or writer had the choice of remaining anonymous—or of using a pseudonym—at the time his material was originally published in the prison publication.

The fact that many of the better articles in the penal press are reprinted by other penal publications again and again (and occasionally without credit to the original source) made tracing the genealogy of some articles difficult. In spite of utmost care, there is still a possibility of errors. If such be the case, I can only hope for the sympathetic understanding of the offended party.

My deepest appreciation is extended to all those who provided assistance during the research and writing phases of this project. These include the 413 busy prison administrators who responded to my survey, and my hosts (and hostess) during my visits to penal institutions: Warden E. L. Maxwell and Associate Warden John Canney of the Ohio Penitentiary; Miss Marguerite Givens, Supervisor of Education at the Federal Reformatory for Women, Alderson, West Virginia; Assistant Warden James Jordan, Maryland state penitentiary; C. D. List, Supervisor of Education at the United States Penitentiary at Terre Haute, Indiana; Dan Orewiler, Director of Classification, Indiana Reformatory; and Herbert Gerdemann, Supervisor of Printing, Illinois state prison at Menard.

Special thanks are also due to Edwin L. Kennedy, whose Baker Award Fund at Ohio University provided resources for salary and travel during the final stages of this study; to Professor Howard B. Gill, Director of the Institute of Correctional Administration at American University, who read the entire manuscript and gave especially valuable suggestions; to graduate assistants Jon Engellener, who aided in gathering data during the first year, and John Penrose and Geoffrey McGuire, who provided aid during later stages; to Herman K. Spector, Librarian, San Quentin prison, and Allen Hoffard, Public Information Officer, Bureau of Prisons, for their helpful advice and materials; to Harold Merklen, Research Librarian, New York Public Library;

James J. Heslin, director of the New York Historical Society; Jon Pankake, Assistant Curator, Public Communications Department, Minnesota Historical Society; and Margaret Gleason, Reference Librarian, The State Historical Society of Wisconsin, for their aid in the search for historical data.

Above all, a very special note of appreciation to the editors of penal publications whose story this is: May their sentences be short.

R. N. B.

Athens, Ohio

December 11, 1966

The Penal Press

CHAPTER 1

The Penal Press and Its Community

A large prison is a community. It contains humor, tragedy, drama and a peculiar culture of its own. And communication is a vital part of any community, inside or outside the walls. . . .—The INSIDER, D.C. Jail, September, 1965

THE OFFICE of the *OPNews,* the inmate newspaper of the Ohio Penitentiary, is not much different in appearance from a newspaper office in any small American town. As you approach it, you see a large plain sign to the right of the door that proclaims that this is the "town" newspaper. (Pentown, as it is called, has a population on this day of 4,572. The editors never have any difficulty with the population figure; it is verified by daily counts.) One of the differences that can be noticed immediately is another, smaller sign, laboriously carved from wood, that hangs from the door. The sign's intricacy suggests that time

3

must have a different meaning in this community; someone must have spent endless hours in carving, sanding, and varnishing the letters that spell "OPNews."

Inside the office, the scene is also largely typical of small-town newspapers. Three staff members, all men, sit at scarred desks pecking away at their middle-aged typewriters. It is Thursday, and the issue to be delivered to readers on Friday has just come off the press. Because these three men constitute the entire full-time staff, work has already begun on next week's edition; unlike some of their outside-world counterparts, this staff cannot take press day as a rest period before pushing ahead with next week's issue. Although there are a few voluntary contributors who send in some news items, the editors need every day of the week to put these items into publishable prose, write the headlines, compose the editorials, and cover all the events of Pentown.

Space in the office is at a premium; nevertheless, a narrow plank cot takes up some room along one wall. The workday is long, starting at daybreak and often extending long after sundown. Brief respites on the cot provide time for meditation and planning, or for recharging mental processes. Above the cot, near one end, a framed certificate awarded to the newspaper for "special excellence" in 1961 is displayed.

There is an obvious eagerness on the part of the staff members to put out a quality newspaper and to win recognition. Their talk revolves around ways in which the last issue could have been better, new headlines, the space allocated to sports, and other changes which might improve their product. The fact that only one award—this time for a story written by a contributor—came to them in the current year's contests brings out some complaints about the judging. But the complaints quickly give way to enthusiasm and pride as they bring out back issues that had seemed especially good.

Fighting for space with large steam pipes along the wall opposite the cot are shelves containing bound volumes of a small number of the back issues from the paper's seventy-five-year history. These volumes and the loaded file cabinet—all within easy reach of the desks—complete the furnishings of the office.

Conspicuously absent is the customary clatter from presses and machinery in a back shop. Instead of being located behind the editorial office, the print shop is in another building some distance away.

But, aside from the fact that it is in a different location, there is little about the shop that would distinguish it from any other. The usual variety of equipment is on hand, and its state of antiquity is typical. The pride and joy of the shop is the newly acquired Model 31 Linotype which now permits the setting of a wide variety of Spartan Gothic headlines. Last week's issue proudly announced this new acquisition.

Thus, in many ways, the *OPNews* is like any town's newspaper. But there are differences, and these make the *OPNews* and all other penal publications a unique segment of America's fourth estate.

One striking difference is in the background of the paper's staff. All full-time members (editor, feature editor, and sports editor) are convicted felons paying a debt of time to the state. The *OPNews* editor is a longtime resident of his community. Now forty years old, he entered its gates fifteen years earlier to serve a life sentence for murder. Some experience in Pentown's print shop, an interest in writing and self-improvement, and confidence of prison officials in his ability to do the job resulted in his appointment as editor fifteen months previously. Neither he nor the other members of the staff have had journalistic training.

THE PRISON COMMUNITY

The contrasts between a prison community and an outside one are as striking as those between this staff and the professionally trained journalists who man outside newspapers. Gray stone walls, dotted at the top with guard towers, surround the community. Access to the outside world is denied by force, and the residents of this community must live an unnatural life in a walled-off society.

Their life is one of maximum security, in every sense of the term. They do not have to be concerned about their subsistence needs. Food, clothing, and shelter are provided for them. There are doctors and a 150-bed hospital to care for their illnesses. They are guaranteed work. Unless they desire to do so, there is no need for them to exercise their mentalities. All aspects of life are planned for them.

Thus, the basic audience of the three editors is composed of men who, like themselves, could not live under the minimum rules of the

free society into which they were born, and now must live under
maximum regimentation in a society whose very structure breeds fear,
frustration, and despair.[1] An authoritarian outside force, armed and in
firm control, imposes upon them a code of conduct that encompasses
every detail of daily life.[2]

Life for the inmates consequently is one of bells, buzzers, orders,
passes, and "shakedowns." They awaken to the ringing of a bell, go to
bed at the sound of a bell. They are counted and recounted. Any
departure from normal routine requires a special pass. Virtually every
moment of the waking day is spent under the watchful surveillance of
armed guards. After the lights-out bell, they must sleep so the night
guard can see a part of their bodies outside the covers. Their
possessions are strictly limited, and perpetual shakedowns guarantee
that unauthorized materials do not come into their possession.

Under the law, prisoners have few rights—to be clothed, fed,
housed, and provided with medical care. All other concessions are
merely privileges granted by prison officials. Any violation of regulations can quickly bring revocation of privileges, isolation, transfer to a
less desirable job assignment, or additional time in confinement. The
prison court is quick and efficient in enforcing the regulations spelled
out with precision in the inmate manual.

But another code is also in force.[3] This one is, in some respects, even
more feared. Each convict knows that, unwritten though it may be, the
social code imposed by his peers is backed by fearful powers of
enforcement. He knows that anything from ostracism to physical vio-

1. There are numerous excellent sociological studies of the prison community. Especially helpful for journalists and others without a background
in penology is a collection of such studies, *The Sociology of Punishment and
Correction*, ed. Norman Johnston, *et al.* (New York: John Wiley & Sons,
1962). Item 14 in the collection, "The Inmate Social Code and Its Functions,"
by Gresham Sykes and Sheldon L. Messinger, is an excellent description of
the structure and problems of a prison society. Also see Donald Clemmer,
The Prison Community (Boston: Christopher Publishing House, 1940).

2. Department of Mental Hygiene and Correction, State of Ohio, *Inmate
Manual, Handbook of Information and Regulations Governing Men Committed
to the Ohio State Penitentiary* (Columbus: Ohio Penal Industries, 1961). Also
see Board of Control of State Institutions, *Rule Book: Iowa State Penitentiary* (Fort Madison, 1961), for a stricter set of rules.

3. Johnston, *op. cit.*

lence can come to him if he defies this code which, in essence, is a direct antithesis to the regulations of his captors. Even the most hardened prisoner must find it discomforting that his constant companions are murderers, rapists, thieves, and sexual deviants, and that he is subject to their judgment and concepts of justice.

Add to the dichotomy between official and unofficial authority the loss of self-identity that comes from being a number instead of a person, the severe psychological and physiological pressures of a unisexual existence, the loss of normal emotional supports from family and friends, and you have the basic components of prison society. Publication of a newspaper or magazine for this kind of a community is fraught with problems large and small, tangible and intangible.

Censorship, for example, is ever present in a walled-off society. The three members of the *OPNews* staff mentioned earlier understand and accept, though sometimes grudgingly, the fact that all their material must be read and approved by the associate warden and the warden's administrative assistant. An obvious effort on the part of Ohio Penitentiary Warden E. L. Maxwell and his associates to allow the *OPNews* to be as much of an inmate periodical as possible makes the censorship less obtrusive and less objectionable. In spite of what would seem to be the obvious necessity for administrative controls over editorial content, many prison editors are quick to voice resentment over such controls. In the main, however, they are realistic. Editor Martin Snyder of the Leavenworth Penitentiary *New Era* expressed it neatly when he wrote:

> There are some cons who would applaud us if we used our venom on the administration, judges, parole system, etc. No can do. The administration, after all, owns the bats and balls and gloves—and stadium.[4]

Pragmatic though they may be about this issue, prison editors, nevertheless, are faced with the conflict between inmate pressures for crusading and the ever present administrative lid on their efforts. Somehow they must win inmate approval without blowing off the lid and losing their publication.

4. Martin Snyder, "Editorial," *New Era*, XVIII (Summer, 1964), 4.

There are numerous other problems, too. Budgets are minimal in almost every instance. Equipment is usually insufficient, outdated, or in demand for other government printing jobs. Maintenance of an experienced staff is difficult; an editor cannot simply hire one. As a matter of fact, he probably has not the slightest influence in its selection. And the only background he can be certain his staff will have is a criminal record. In reality, selection of staff is determined by chance, criminal activity, a judge, and the prison's administration. Its tenure is set by these outside sources, plus a parole board, and *not* by the needs of the publication. As one editor facetiously put it, "I've never had a staff member stay beyond his sentence, no matter how much we needed him. Come to think of it, I won't either."

In spite of the abundance of problems associated with prison publications work, penal press jobs are prized by those who have them. Staff members are convinced that the advantages and special privileges of their work outweigh the disadvantages of the assignment. Chief among these advantages is an intangible—the feeling of recognition and importance that editorship and authorship can bring. In the words of Al Rutledge, editor of the Maryland Penitentiary *Courier*, "A prisoner is a nothing. He's just a vegetable. Anything that gives him identity has a value beyond measure. And that's what editing the *Courier* does for me, it makes me somebody." This contribution to self-identity, self-satisfaction, and individual pride is one of the greatest advantages cited by penal editors.

Other advantages are of a more minor nature, at least from the viewpoint of an outsider, and they vary considerably from institution to institution. Behind walls anywhere, however, the most minute and routine details of life take on special significance, and sometimes values can turn topsy-turvy. For instance (referring once again to the *OPNews* staff), the long hours worked by the editors are considered an advantage. All three editors can be relatively sure of putting in the maximum 200 hours a month permitted by the institution. At their four-cent hourly wage rate, they may earn $8.00 a month. Half of this is set aside for their release date, but the remainder can be spent for such "essential non-essentials" as tobacco. Prisoners working in other shops often accumulate less paid time each month, and in the convict world a few cents can mean a pack of cigarettes, and a pack of cigarettes can take on tremendous importance in the "cigarette economy" of prison society.[5]

Another valued privilege of assignment to the *OPNews* is some freedom of movement within the prison. In this and other maximum security institutions, inmates ordinarily cannot move from one area to another except when they march in groups under guard. The three editors have been cleared for access to all areas within the inner gate. They are also permitted to enter the dining hall individually and ahead of the marching groups. The 5:00 P.M. lock-up time (when most prisoners are locked in their cells) is waived for the editors. They are permitted to work in the newspaper office until 9:00 P.M. and are granted the special privilege of a sandwich at that time.

Not all prison publications nor all correctional institutions are identical with the examples cited here; local variations exist. Administrations differ as to privileges that are granted. Basic inmate rules vary, even in maximum security institutions. In juvenile and minimum or medium security institutions, daily routines vary considerably.

Publications differ, too. They adopt different formats and approaches to their goals. As a result, their problems vary to some extent. The editor of a quarterly literary magazine faces challenges dissimilar to those of the editor of a weekly newspaper. Nevertheless, the problems, goals, successes, and failures of the press in all correctional institutions must and do have basic similarities because the underlying societal structure in which they operate is the same.

THE BASIS FOR A PRISON PRESS

The mere existence of any kind of a press in penal communities is remarkable. Publication of newspapers and magazines—instruments of freedom and individual expression—indicates at least two things. First of all, it reveals an obvious fact to which the penal press often

5. M. Arc, "The Prison 'Culture'—From the Inside," *New York Times Magazine*, February 28, 1965, p. 53. This is the unusual account of an anthropologist who served a sentence in a federal correctional institution. The situation provided the rare opportunity for a scholar to combine his objective outlook with the subjective feelings of the prisoner.

directs the attention of outside readers: prisoners, though outcasts from society, are, after all, still human beings with definite needs for information, communication with others, and outlets for creative self-expression. Secondly, it indicates the existence of enlightened and persevering institutional administrations, because periodic publication of the printed word immediately bodes trouble and extra work for those who must maintain a secure, orderly society.

Perhaps, in the final analysis, it is the willingness of prison administrators to foster newspapers and magazines in their institutions that is the most unusual aspect of the prison press. The penal press is an anomaly; authoritarian rule and the printing press historically have been incompatible. And the very confinement of men to prison is, in its essence, a denial of their liberty. In the world of American prisons, however, as paradoxical as it may seem, the indulgence of those in authority, plus the seemingly irrepressible desire of their captives to write, to communicate, and to create, have fostered a fascinating branch of the fourth estate that has unusual scope, vigor, and importance.

SCOPE AND GENERAL CHARACTERISTICS
OF THE PENAL PRESS

The scope of the penal press in terms of numbers, types, and circulation has been the subject of a guessing game in penal publications for years. Normally, a profession's active participants gather data about their professional activity, but the inability of penal editors to meet with one another and to communicate on an inter-institutional basis has hampered accurate compilations.

An intensive search by letter, questionnaire, telephone, and personal interview during 1965 and 1966 brought, for this study, some form of response from officials of 91.3 per cent of the state and federal correctional institutions in the fifty states.[6] Through the cooperation of

6. The American Correctional Association, *Directory of State and Federal Correctional Institutions* (Washington: The American Correctional Association, August, 1965), was used for the mailing list. Only institutions from the fifty states were polled. A follow-up form letter, then a personal letter were

institution administrators and convict editors, basic data were collected on 222 general inmate publications. A list of these publications, with some basic details about them, is presented in Appendix A. In addition, the existence of 113 special interest inmate publications was verified. These included magazines and newspapers produced by Alcoholics Anonymous, Dale Carnegie, and the Junior Chamber of Commerce, along with religious groups, drug-addict groups, and others. In several instances, these were the only publications produced in an institution, and will be discussed separately in Chapter 4.

Numerous statistics concerning the scope of inmate publications were gathered in this survey, and these data are presented in detail in Appendix B. It will suffice here to give a basic summary.

More than half (53.7 per cent) of the correctional institutions in the United States have inmate publications. Existence of these publications depends to some extent, of course, on the size and character of the institution. Forestry camps with a population numbering 20 or 30 could not be expected to produce a newspaper or magazine. Nevertheless, in institutions of under 500 inmates, more than one-third (39.2 per cent) have a publication. At the other extreme, more than three-fourths (77.7 per cent) of those with populations of 1,000 or more have publications. In total, because institutions with publications tend to be larger, 65.5 per cent of the inmates of correctional institutions have publications representing them. The fact that in some states one publication serves several institutions also causes the percentage of inmates receiving publications to be larger than the percentage of institutions with publications.

It is interesting to note that *every* federal penitentiary, reformatory, and juvenile institution has a publication, and all but two of the federal group called "correctional institutions" have publications. Only a few short-term diagnostic and pre-release guidance centers are without

---

used after the first group of responses were in. Finally, a rough-draft listing of publications was mailed to all responding institutions, asking for verification of their listing and for information about penal publications not listed. The few publications in county or municipal jails were turned up in this fashion; they were not intended to be fully explored in this study. All data summarizing characteristics of the penal press presented in this volume are from this questionnaire and from personal interviews in depth at selected institutions, unless otherwise specified.

them. Although larger budgets are undoubtedly a factor in the almost universal use of inmate publications by federal institutions, encouragement from top executives has probably helped, too. No formal policy directives from the Bureau of Prisons govern the conduct of inmate publications, but Director Myrl E. Alexander has indicated: "We encourage inmate expression through creative writing. These magazines can be most helpful in providing a medium of communication for inmates." [7]

The total reported circulation of the publications from which data were gathered was 240,036. Of these publications, 80,416 copies were being sent to outside readers either by subscription or on a complimentary basis. If the inmate populations of those institutions not reporting circulation figures are assumed to constitute their circulation, the total audience would be 259,374.

Publications are almost equally divided between magazines and newspapers. This would seem to indicate a division of emphasis between the goals of providing literary outlets and media of general communication. Normally a publication designed to disseminate information is more likely to be produced as a newspaper; a literary outlet usually takes magazine form. In the case of prison publications, however, the content of many is contrary to the norm. Newspapers may be loaded with literary material, and magazines may be full of news. Mechanical facilities, rather than content, often seem to determine the form.

The titles of penal publications show, collectively, some of the basic philosophy, aspirations, pessimism, optimism, and sense of humor of their founders and readers. The first penal publication was the *Forlorn Hope*. At a later date there was a *Star of Hope* and a *Hope Press*. There is, or has been, a *Stretch* magazine, several *Time*[s], a *Time & Tied*, a *Bars and Stripes*, an *Encourager*, an *Eye Opener*, two *About Face*[s], a *New Leaf*, a *New Era*, a *Cross Roads*, a *Palace of Kings*, and an *Insider*. Many have prosaic names; others have such inexplicable titles as *Enchanted News*, *Tiki*, and *Acorn*.

The range of quality, both in content and physical appearance, is extreme. At the one pole are the small, unpretentious, amateurish

7. Letter from Allen Hoffard, Public Information Officer, Bureau of Prisons, Washington, D. C., April 15, 1966.

mimeographed or spirit-duplicated periodicals in the low-population juvenile institutions. A case in point is a school for delinquent ten- to fourteen-year-olds that produces more than one publication in order to get maximum participation of its residents. The enterprising teachers at the school are hard-pressed to find among their charges enough literates to fill their little newspapers with semi-grammatical offerings, let alone to create a polished product. But the stumbling efforts of these uneducated delinquents to communicate verbally represent a monumental achievement for them and their teachers. Under the circumstances, these publications may be more constructive in the rehabilitative process than the more sophisticated efforts in some adult prisons.

The main concern in this study is, however, the newspapers and magazines of adult penal institutions. Here one finds publications of exceptional quality, as well as some rather elementary efforts. Such magazines as the *New Era,* of the federal penitentiary at Leavenworth, are as attractive as any first-class magazine on the outside, and their content is of high quality, too. *New Era,* which has drawn favorable comment from *Saturday Review,*[8] is a literary quarterly, standard (8½ x 11 inches) size, that has contained as many as 104 pages. Another slick quarterly is the *Raiford Record* of the Florida State Prison. Its excellence was recognized in 1963 when it was awarded the "Maggie" of the Florida Magazine Association as the best magazine in the state.[9] In a poll of prison editors conducted by *Saturday Review* in 1963, the Atlanta Federal Penitentiary's *Atlantian,* also a quarterly literary magazine, won top position.[10] In these and other top-level penal magazines, the essays, short stories, cartoons, and fact articles on prison-related and non-prison topics are meticulously presented. One would think, in appraising them, that their publishers had selected staffs from the finest literary talent available and had used only the most skilled graphic arts craftsmen in their production.

Among newspapers, one of the foremost is the *Menard Time,* a

8. James F. Fixx, "Journalists Behind Bars," *Saturday Review,* March 9, 1963, p. 55.

9. Letter from E. C. Frick, *Florida Newspaper News and Radio Digest,* to R. E. Upton, Jr., Director of Education, Raiford Prison, Raiford, Florida, August 15, 1963.

10. Fixx, *op. cit.,* p. 57.

monthly tabloid (*New York Daily News, Chicago Sun-Times* size) of the Illinois State Penitentiary, Menard Branch. The *Time* was selected as the best prison newspaper in the country in 1966 by judges of the American Penal Press Contest, a national contest sponsored by Southern Illinois University. Not even the most recently founded suburban tabloid, using every modern facility for its publication, would surpass the *Menard Time* in appearance. The quality of its news presentation and its editorial judgment, even in an instance when violence occurred in the prison, have brought unusual recognition from political and journalistic sources.

Many others have their own unique claims to distinction. Some, like the *Enchanted News* of New Mexico State Penitentiary, are known for multi-color artwork of exceptional beauty. This is done by silk screening, a process that is rarely feasible for outside magazines because it is too time-consuming. The ancient art of hand setting type is still preserved, not only by the *Enchanted News* but also by the *Presidio*, the Iowa State Penitentiary's magazine, and several other smaller publications. Commercial periodicals, since the invention of the Linotype and other line-casting machines, could not consider setting each individual letter and character by hand. Thus, some of the skill and artistry of the primitive graphic arts are being preserved by prison publications because, for them, time is cheap.

In the Shelby County (Tennessee) jail, a staff produces the only known daily of the penal press. From the reformatory at Elmira, New York, comes a newspaper that declares in its nameplate that it is the oldest penal publication in the world. Another publication, that of the Massachusetts Correctional Institution at Concord, is labeled the oldest in terms of continual publication. Others chauvinistically point with pride to similar marks of distinction. The real backbone of the penal press, however, is the large group of papers and magazines that do not win many prizes, but are good, solid, substantial publications of excellent quality. Newspapers like the *OPNews*, the *San Quentin News*, the *Spectator* of Southern Michigan Prison, the *Prison Mirror* at Stillwater, Minnesota, and the *Mentor* of the Massachusetts Correctional Institution at Walpole are not "flashy," but they serve their communities exceptionally well. Content of the mimeographed *Terrescope* of

Terre Haute Federal Penitentiary and *Stretch* of Kansas State Prison is as good as, or better than, their more spectacularly printed counterparts.

A point of pride for most of these publications is their membership in an organization called the Penal Press. With only its capital letters to distinguish it from the generic description of the prison press, the Penal Press is a strange organization, half real and half unreal. It is somewhat like the Associated Press and other news-gathering associations. It is also similar to the American Society of Newspaper Editors and bears some resemblance to syndicates such as the Newspaper Enterprise Association. Although it performs the functions of these "free world" journalistic organizations and, consequently, is in some ways similar, the Penal Press actually is like nothing else in existence. It is, in the words of *San Quentin News* Editor Cary Johanneson, a "fictional fact." [11] Its membership is made up of convicts and their publications, yet its entire existence and success depend on honor only. There are no officers, no headquarters, no dues, no conventions, no service fees, no rules, and no means of enforcing rules, even if there were any. But its members display its label as proudly as the outside press proclaims its memberships and services. And, in many respects, it does its job more efficiently and successfully than other press associations, syndicates, and editors' groups.

Members of the Penal Press grant to other members the right to reprint their material, but credit must be given to the original source. Failure to give such credit quickly brings published criticism of the offender. Such violations of the Penal Press code are considered to be serious breaches of honor, and every effort is made to keep them to a minimum.

Some Penal Press members have attempted, with little success, to add status and stability to their organization by formalizing a code and credo. Basically it is only the determination of most prison editors to give their "organization" substance that prevents it from being completely nebulous. It is this determination of editors to accomplish

11. Cary Johanneson, "A Fictional Fact," *San Quentin News*, April 14, 1966, p. 2.

something worthwhile, and the willingness of prison officials to permit them to try it, that has made the press in correctional institutions a factor of considerable consequence.

There is potential for the penal press to make contributions in a number of ways: as an internal communications medium transmitting useful information to the inmate population and to official personnel; as an external medium making the public aware of problems faced both by convicts and prison administrators; as an educational experience for staff members and a morale booster for inmates; and as an outlet for creative self-expression and aid toward rehabilitation.

How valuable is the penal press in these areas? There has not been complete agreement among prison officials, sociologists, and psychologists on the answer to this question. Not only is there some disagreement with regard to each specific function, but there is also some disagreement as to whether, in total, penal press accomplishments merit its existence. As one warden put it, "Reasons for our not having an inmate publication are too numerous to mention." Yet the steady spread of penal publications indicates that, although they once were the exception, they are tending to become the rule. Problems of financing, of time for administering them, of disagreements over content, of distribution, of potential plagiarism, and of special privileges needed if a staff is to put together a good publication are enough to force penal publications to constantly prove their worth. Their tenacity indicates at least a reasonable success in providing that proof.

CHAPTER 2

Origins of Prison Publications

. . . it is my will that Imprisonment for Debt, *be done away, and the debtor's prisons, in different parts of this State, those human slaughter houses, be converted into seminaries of learning for the advancement of human happiness . . .*—From "The Last Will and Testament of a Debtor," FORLORN HOPE, Vol. I, No. 1, New York Prison, March 24, 1800.

THE PENAL PRESS was born in 1800, a year of particular significance in American history. Signaling the start of a new century, the year seemed to be pregnant with change. The national capital was moved from New York to its permanent location at Washington. Most importantly, national leadership passed from the Federalists, who had guided the new democracy from its inception, to the Jeffersonian Republicans. As representatives of rank-and-file Americans who feared that a new tyranny was developing, Jefferson and his followers were

17

swept into office on a wave of sentiment for basic freedoms, including freedom of the press.

The Jeffersonians won much of their support as the result of their fight for the inclusion of a Bill of Rights in the Constitution and their opposition to the Alien and Sedition Acts of 1798. Administration of these acts by the Federalists had resulted in the prosecution of several anti-Federalists who had written or spoken against the government. In coffee houses, homes, taverns, and wherever else people gathered, talk centered on the basic rights of the individual (whether unpropertied or wealthy). Always, the freedom to publish newspapers of dissent emerged as a cornerstone of all other freedoms.

This saturation of the public mind with thoughts of freedoms, rights, and privileges perhaps accounted for the phenomenon of publication of a prison newspaper at such an early date in our history. Certainly there was nothing about the prison administration of those days that would have encouraged an inmate publication; although some advancements were being made, penology was still in its dark ages.[1]

1. Richard R. Korn and Lloyd McCorkle, *Criminology and Penology* (New York: Henry Holt & Company, 1959). See Chap. 16, "A Selective History of Penal Rationales and Procedures." About ten years before the founding of *Forlorn Hope*, the Pennsylvania state legislature had reinstated the essentials of the "Great Law" of the Quaker Assembly of 1682, which had provided for imprisonment as a basic means of punishment instead of various forms of "torture." Provision for some separation according to age, sex, and seriousness of offense was also an advancement for that era. But the essential part of the "Pennsylvania System," as it finally emerged in 1829 with the completion of the Eastern Penitentiary in Philadelphia, was solitary confinement, an element of punishment that has been subject to much criticism. The next major change in penology came with the building of a prison at Auburn, New York, in 1823. Here a system of working together in silence was permitted for convicts. This working together was considered an advancement over solitary confinement, but to insure absolute silence inmates were forbidden to look at one another face to face. It was thought that this would lead to gestures, then to whispering, then to talking. When moving about in groups, inmates placed one hand on the shoulder of the man in front and marched with a short, heavy stride known as the *lockstep*. Silence and the lockstep were earmarks of what became known as the "Auburn System." Neither the Pennsylvania System nor the Auburn System contained any concept of penology that would have tended to give encouragement or support to the establishment of an inmate newspaper.

THE *FORLORN HOPE*, FIRST PENAL NEWSPAPER

America's first penal newspaper was founded by an inmate of the New York Prison. His goal was to work for the enactment of a bankruptcy law. Imprisoned along with hundreds of others because he could not satisfy his creditors, William Keteltas established the *Forlorn Hope* on Monday, March 24, 1800, in an effort to bring an end to imprisonment for debt in the United States.[2]

Forlorn Hope survived less than a year, the last known edition being September 13, 1800. During his six months of publishing, Keteltas crusaded for prison reform in general, but he concentrated on imprisonment for debt as a prime evil. Page one of his first issue (Figure 1) was typical of his product. It contained a salutatory message (which was repeated in the same position in the second issue), an extract from the New York Constitution along with editorial comment that imprisonment for debt could not be justified under the state constitution, a last will and testament of a Revolutionary War officer bitterly offering his dead body for sale to satisfy his creditors, and a personal note from Keteltas to his creditors vowing his determination to pay his debts if ever permitted the freedom to work and earn the necessary funds.

Page one of issue Number Two of *Forlorn Hope* contained the same salutatory message and constitutional extracts, followed by the first installment of a reprint of George Washington's Farewell Address, which it took Keteltas three issues to complete.

Forlorn Hope consisted of four 10 x 17-inch pages published weekly on Saturday. There were three columns to a page. Page four was devoted to advertisements which, along with outside subscriptions, provided the financial support for the venture. The middle two pages contained a miscellany including, for example, a long poem bemoaning the imprisonment of war veterans for debt stemming from war service; a list of toasts that could be said while drinking to elimination

2. The only known copy of the first issue of *Forlorn Hope* is in the library of the Wisconsin Historical Society, bound with a volume of miscellaneous Albany newspapers. The Library of Congress Rare Book Room has the second issue (March 31, 1800) to September 6, 1800. The New York Historical Society has March 31 and April 19 to September 13, 1800.

Forlorn Hope.

WASHINGTON'S EXAMPLE WILL BREAK THE CHAIN.

SOFT SMILING HOPE! THOU ANCHOR OF THE MIND,   ALL LOOK TO THEE, WHEN SORROW WRINGS THE HEART,
AND ONLY COMFORT WHICH THE WRETCHED FIND—   TO SOOTHE, BY FUTURE PROSPECTS, PRESENT SMART.

VOL. I.]   PRISON, NEW-YORK——MONDAY, MARCH 24, 1800.   [NUM. I.

TO THE PUBLIC.

THE love of liberty is the strongest passion of the human soul! To indulge it no sacrifice is thought too great—no price too dear, to him, who has felt its generous flame. As man grew in stature, his first thoughts and exertions were, and still are, devoted to the enjoyment of this divine gift. Millions, countless millions of the human race, have bled and still bleed, from the earliest age to this very moment, for this gratification. Even death looses its terrors when opposed to this celestial fire! it is unconquerable, and will not stop short of a reunion with the fountain of light and life, from whence it flowed to man.

Restrained in this enjoyment, with many, too many of my fellow citizens in the different prisons in this state, and finding myself at the mercy of an individual, I fly to the constitution—the ark of safety. I ask the Representatives of the people, to whom is intrusted the application of its preserving power, to apply the remedy by a law for our deliverance? To point out the necessity of legislative interference, I need only relate the devastation of property and the destruction of lives, lost by the operation of a law intended to have a contrary effect. Finding it impossible to do this by a petition, as forcibly as through the medium of a paper, I have determined to attempt the establishment of one, for this express purpose, of which this is a specimen, and will accompany proposals to obtain subscriptions for its support.

WILLIAM KETELTAS.

Extract from the Constitution of the State of New-York.

[LAWS NEW-YORK, VOL. I page 3.]

" WE hold these truths to be self-evident, that all men are created equal, that they are endowed by their Creator, with certain unalienable rights, that among these are life, liberty, and the pursuit of happiness—That to secure these rights, governments are instituted amongst men, deriving their just powers from the consent of the governed ; that when any form of government becomes destructive of these ends, it is the right of the people, to alter or abolish it, and to institute new government, laying its foundation on such principles, and organizing its powers in such form, as to them shall seem most likely to effect their safety and happiness."

Extract from Vol. 1st. page 408, Laws of New-York.—Plaintiff may have execution against the body or estate of the Debtor, &c.

And further, That every person who hath been, or shall hereafter be taken or arrested, by virtue of any such writ or execution, against his or her body, for any such debt or damages, by any Sheriff, or other Officer to whom any such writ hath been or shall be directed : And every person who hath been, or shall be committed to the custody of any Sheriff or other Officer, in execution, for any such debt or damages, shall be safely kept in prison, in close and secure custody, *without bail or mainprize, living at his or her own costs*, until he or she shall satisfy and pay such debt and damages. And if any such Sheriff or other Officer, shall permit any such person so taken, arrested or committed, to go out of prison or be at large, by bail, mainprize or otherwise, without the assent and agreement of the Plaintiff; such Sheriff or other Officer, shall thereby become answerable to the Plaintiff, for the debt and damages for which such person was taken, arrested or committed ; and the Plaintiff may recover the same with costs, by action of debt, bill or plaint, against such Sheriff or other Officer.

Query. How this law does comport with the above extract from the Constitution, is submitted to the present Legislature.

OBSERVATION.

Were it not for the protection afforded us in the integrity and humanity of our Sheriff and jailer, under whose immediate control we are, the tyranny which creditors might practise on the debtor in confinement, through that medium, is incalculable.

An interested number of Debtors.

THE LAST WILL AND TESTAMENT OF A DEBTOR.

IN the name of God, how can these things be ? I, A. L. being of sound mind and memory, but feeble in body, owing to imprisonment for a great length of time, Do make, ordain and publish this as my Last Will and Testament. Having witnessed the dissolution of several of my fellow-citizens and companions, in close confinement occasioned by the insupportable miseries attending this wretched condition of human nature ; and finding my own dissolution fast approaching by the gradual decay of my body, think it my duty, as life is uncertain to make this last effort to pay my unfortunate creditors.

1st. As to lands, tenements, goods and chattels, I have none.

2d. My soul I resign to Almighty God, who gave it me, being ever disposed that the rightful owner should have what belongs to him.

3d. After it is clearly ascertained, that my soul is separated from the body, which, by a law of this state, is the property of my creditors, if it meets their wishes, it is my will, it should be offered for sale to the surgeons of this city, by my Executors, hereafter named, to satisfy their just demands against me, and the monies arising therefrom, be loaned at lawful interest, and the interest to be applied to their several demands, which are few and trifling, and within the compass of payment, by adopting this only, this awful alternative.

4th. Having got through with the disposition, of the only material thing I have to dispose of, I proceed to dispose of a political right, the only thing left, which I value more for what it cost, than the good it ever has done me, but ought to be considered of great worth to a free people.

5th. As I have a right by the constitution of this State, to express my opinion for the public good, and in all probability, being the last time I shall ever exercise it, is my will that *Imprisonment for Debt*, be done

away, and the debtor's prisons, in different parts of this State, those human slaughter houses, be converted into seminaries of learning for the advancement of human happiness and not sacrifice.

6th. May the Legislature of this State imitate the patriotic majorities in the New-Jersey and Pennsylvania Legislatures, who have already done away imprisonment for debt as tyrannical, unjust and inhuman, and unbecoming the character of a free people.

7th. By the constitution of this State, it is declared " that all men are born equal, and have certain unalienable rights, viz—Life, Liberty, and the pursuits of Happiness."

8th. Under this constitution, may never another of Columbia's sons be deprived of this constitutional right as I am at present, with upwards of 100 more of my unfortunate fellow-citizens now confined in the goal of this city ; but enjoy, under a rightful administration of this constitution, what the blood of our fathers was shed to secure to us and our posterity.

9th. May succeeding legislatures prevent one citizen from destroying another, by imprisoning him for debt, in violation of the letter and spirit of this constitution.

10th. May the debtor's property be amenable to the creditors and not the imprisonment of his person, which pays no debts.

11th. A uniform system of Bankruptcy, by the general government, a law essential to the interest, honour and happiness of a free people.

12th. In founding the American republic, I was among the first, to sacrifice my fortune and risque my life, supposing my country was about to be enslaved ; all the advantages I have gained by my sacrifices, I hope my children will never inherit.

13th. As there is no difference, in my opinion, between the operation of the ca sa in this state, and the late lettres de cachet in France when a despotism, it is my will it should be destroyed here as it was in France, when she became a Republic.

14th. May the virulence of party spirit subside among the people, and a decent respect for the opinions of each other, restore that harmony and union among them, without which they cannot long be free.

15th. Those of my creditors who have destroyed me from malice or ignorance, I sincerely forgive, upon condition they receive their just demands from my executors, arising from the sale of my deceased body, that no reflections may be cast on my innocent widow and children.

16th. Washington's example I bequeath my countrymen, as the richest legacy ; while followed, will be a barrier against every public and private vice.

To carry this my last will and testament into effect, I appoint and make choice of A. B. and C. D. my executors, for their strict attachment to their interest, presuming, as they paid such attention to my body when alive, to obtain their money, they will not forsake it, when dead, but will dispose of it to the best advantage to satisfy their demands.

An old American Officer.

D. M.
E. J. } Witnesses,
J. J.

For the Forlorn Hope.

To my Creditors,

WHEN the language of affection is not permitted to vent itself, the human heart resembles a depot or reservoir, where a continual addition of tributary streams, pour their increasing supply into the general stock ; till denied the opportunity of passing off, and the supply be continued, will it not either rise over all its mounds, or ultimately destroy its banks with overwhelming fury ? Like causes produce like effects. These reflections result from having made several fruitless efforts to convey (through a newspaper channel) to mistaken creditors, the distressed situation I am placed in. Deprived by unavoidable misfortune of my all, yet not without sincere intentions (should it please Providence, to crown my future endeavours with success) to pay all I owe.

FIGURE 1

The first issue of America's first prison newspaper. (From the files of the Wisconsin Historical Society.)

of debt imprisonment; an essay-obituary signed *Edwardus* and lamenting the death in prison of a friend whose only crime was to owe money; a line drawing of the prison; a few items of foreign and domestic news; a list of Republican political candidates; an item on a ship-launching; a list of typographical errors in previous issues; an apology for failure to deliver the previous issue; the conclusion of Washington's Farewell Address; a portion of a Frenchman's essay on crime and punishment; a notice of the bravery of a Negro in fighting a French privateer only to end up in prison (with comments on the injustice of slavery); and the following two items, a letter to the editor and a poem, reprinted here in their entirety:

> Mr. Editor.
> Please to insert the following laconic but impressive letter from a mother to her son, the only prop of her declining life in a strange land, (from misfortune divided and living in different states) with his laconic answer.
> Dear Son,
> I am in Goal [Jail].
>   Yours & c.
> Dear Mother,
> God help you, so am I.
>   Yours & c.
>
> Says John to his friend, "What is't to be free?"
> "Why to live in a country by Congress decree,
> The nation most free and enlighten'd on earth,
> For liberty here is secur'd from our birth."
>
> John replied "Is this so? Well, we'll see in a crack."
> And without proof of debt, clapp'd a writ on his back;
> Had him taken to jail, for the lawyers—he feed 'em,
> And there left him to boast of his excellent freedom.
>
>   R.E.[3]

However forlorn his newspaper, there can be no doubt about Mr. Keteltas' singleness of purpose and devotion to a cause. What brought about the end of *Forlorn Hope* is not known, but references to changes in printers, and the normal financial problems of newspapers depending upon advertising and subscriptions in those days, would lead to a

3. *Forlorn Hope*, April 19, 1800, pp. 2, 3.

conclusion that the cost perhaps exceeded the revenue. At any rate, its publisher would have been pleased, had he been alive, to have seen passage of the Federal Bankruptcy Act of 1898, a law that would have eliminated the need for a *Forlorn Hope*.

There were basic differences between the *Forlorn Hope* and most prison publications which followed. Apparently prisoner Keteltas acted as an individual entrepreneur in his venture, his publication having no real connection with the prison administration. It also was published for an outside audience, not the inmate population. Hence it was an *external* periodical, whereas most later prison publications got their start basically as *internal* newspapers or magazines.

OTHER PIONEER PRISON PUBLICATIONS

There is no record of any further attempts at prison publications until more than three-quarters of a century later. In the 1880's, three newspapers were founded in rather quick succession, and each is still being published. This triumvirate included the *Summary* of the Elmira Reformatory, New York, in 1883; *Our Paper* of the Massachusetts Correctional Institution, Concord, in 1885; and the *Prison Mirror* of the Minnesota State Penitentiary at Stillwater in 1887.

New concepts in penology probably accounted for the creation of prison newspapers in these institutions at that time. With the introduction of the so-called Elmira System, prisoners were given the opportunity, with good conduct, to earn merits that could shorten their sentences; shops and schools were established; excessive punishment for rule violations was eliminated; and the silent system was relaxed. This more humane outlook on imprisonment originated in Ireland in 1876. It became known as the Elmira System because it was first used for youthful offenders at the New York State Reformatory at Elmira, where the second known prison publication emerged.

The *Summary*

Apparently there are no extant copies of the first nine years of the *Summary* of Elmira Reformatory. Queries to the reformatory, the New

York Public Library, state historical societies in the eastern states, and the Library of Congress produced no information about their existence. There is, in the Library of Congress, Volume 16 (1893); Volume 31 (1913); and Volume 33 (1915).

By 1893, the *Summary* was an impressive publication. Its eight 9½ x 13 inch pages per issue were crammed with a wide variety of material. The first page was usually filled with news of prison reform; page 2 contained a miscellany of reprints from outside newspapers; page 3 included a group of reprints on sociological subjects; page 4 consisted of editorials; page 5 was a digest of the week's news, day by day; page 6 was headed "Potpourri" and included poetry, letters from inmates, and the Delaware, Lackawanna & Western Railroad time table; page 7 contained more national and foreign news; and page 8 was the local page, which included items about inmate promotions and demotions in grade, alumni (Convict 3444 had written from Russia), activities (speeches were summarized), and a program of special events yet to come.

In the January 1, 1893, issue (Figure 2), the *Summary* editorialized for state rather than county care of the insane; against the jailing (in solitary confinement) of an individual pending appeal of his conviction; and against the "snoopy journalism" of outside newspapers that were reporting in detail about the illness of James G. Blaine. Further, there were some comments about a spiritualist claiming proof of the existence of the spirit after it separated from the body; about recent activities of President Cleveland; and about a former editor of the *Summary* who had just been released.

Content of the *Summary* throughout its early years seemed to indicate several purposes for its existence: (1) to speak out editorially for advancements in penology; (2) to summarize major activities related to sociology; (3) to summarize news of the outside world for inmates; (4) to report major happenings within the institution; and (5) to provide an outlet for inmate poetry and prose. With regard to the last objective, the following item indicated that a perennial problem of prison editors was already present in 1893:

> THE SUMMARY will be pleased to receive an occasional contribution from inmates who are capable of writing a good article. In view of the fact that several manuscripts received lately have the

" No man, whatever his offence, ought ever to be discharged from restraint, except upon reasonable evidence that he is morally, intellectually, and physically capable of earning a livelihood."

VOL. XVI., NO. 1.   ELMIRA, N. Y., SUNDAY, JANUARY 1, 1893.   WHOLE NO. 453.

Entered at the Post Office of Elmira, N. Y., as Second Class Matter.

. PRISON REFORM NOTES.

A LETTER has been received from Mr. P. B. Lamoreux, warden of the Wisconsin Prison, stating that he intends to place his institution on a reformative basis and to establish a system of marking similar to that in operation at this Reformatory.

THE GOVERNOR says that an idea should not prevail that the pardoning power is being used more freely than usual. He said : " Gov. Tilden in 1876 granted 160 pardons, Gov. Robinson in 1879 granted 211 pardons, while I have granted but 96 so far this year. The yearly average for each Governor many years back is much more than mine this year."

. WARDEN BROWN, of Sing Sing prison has re-moved sixteen guards, instructors, and keepers who have been employed in that institution. When the prison at Dannemora was burned last summer, the Sing Sing prison had to accommodate more prisoners than there were accommodations for. There are only 1,200 cells, and there were 1,800 prisoners to occupy them. It was necessary to put two in a cell. This necessitated the employing a large number of extra guards and keepers. There are only 1,300 convicts in Sing Sing now, the full gang has been removed to other prisons. The Warden thinks he can get along with fewer employes.

. THE GOVERNOR'S coming message is expected to be an unusually instructive document. He has during the year familiarized himself with every department of the State Government. He has visited penal institutions and lunatic asylums, voyaged along the canal and penetrated the Adirondack wilderness. He was also with the National Guard at Buffalo. The personal knowledge he has gained is expected to make his recommendations of especial value. A published report that Gov. Flower is opposed to capital punishment has brought to him many letters of inquiry and some of congratulation. He is not opposed to the death penalty, however, and will not advocate its abolition.

HITHERTO THE QUESTION of prison discipline and reform has been a matter that has excited little interest and commanded little attention or effort in Arkansas. The State assembly has now, however, about decided to abolish that iniquitous system, the leasing to private individuals or corporations the convict labor of the State ; to effectually abolish those institutions that are now a disgrace to the State: the County Convict Farms of Arkansas ; also to establish a State Reform School for the proper education and restrainment of juvenile offenders, thus keeping them apart from the contamination of hardened criminals and giving them encouragement, so that, when released, they may become good citizens.

THE BALTIMORE NEWS says : It was good tactics on the part of Dr. Ransom of Dannemora prison, N. Y., at the Prison Congress, to rescue the Prison Reformers from the suspicion of being sentimentalists only. He frankly advocated corporal punishment for prisoners. Truly he would not really hurt them overmuch, but he advocates a form of punishment which neatly combines the minimum of physical torture with the maximum of moral suffering. If the moral deterrent effect is all-important, as every Reformer admits, there is but one improvement possible, namely, publicity. In the good old days the pillory shamed more sinners out of open sin than the pulpit managed to persuade. Will Dr. Ransom entertain the friendly suggestion that he amend and strengthen his motion by a clause providing for a public spanking day?

A DETROIT (Michigan) newspaper of late date says : " Among the questions which will come up before the new Board of Supervisors, will be the erection of a new county jail. It is a noto-

rious fact that the Wayne County jail is nothing more than a fire trap. In the event of a fire in the old building there would be a sacrifice of life which would simply be appalling. The outside walls are perfect, but the interior arrangements are very defective. The jail has from time to time been condemned by the inspectors, but no attention has been paid to their reports. In the residence of the Sheriff insects are numerous and the sanitary condition of the building is far from being perfect, although Sheriff Hanley has done his utmost to make the residence as pleasant as possible for the enjoyment of his family. On account of the age of the building it is an impossibility to make it a perfect one in which to live; and therefore it should be improved. Sheriff-elect Collins will take possession of the jail a week from to-night when the midnight bell tolls. His deputies and many of his friends will be present, and an hour will be spent in pleasant social intercourse. In the meantime the residence of the Sheriff will be renovated."

THE MERCER COUNTY JAIL in Trenton, N J., has been visited by smallpox. The authorities refuse to tell any of the particulars of the outbreak. It is known, however, that a colored prisoner of the name of Freeborn Scruby, who has been in the jail for some months, has been stricken with the disease. He was removed promptly to the pest-house outside of the city limits. The pest-house is under guard, and a nurse has been secured. The entire jail has been fumigated, and the warden refuses to expose any more men to the chance of contracting the disease, and, as a consequence, all the prisoners in Trenton and throughout the county are fined instead of being committed to jail. The discovery of the existence of smallpox in the jail was brought about by the refusal of the warden of the jail to receive several Hungarians who had been committed as witnesses. The refusal of the authorities to give any information has given rise to many rumors, but it is believed that but one case of the disease exists

---

THE CAREER OF JAY GOULD.
As viewed by the Class in Ethics.

Could the dead rise from the grave and did but know that which transpires and is being said of them on this sod above their lifeless bodies, Jay Gould would, in all probability, have been an attendant at the Ethics class of the Reformatory last Sunday afternoon where he was being denounced by some, as a deep dyed villain while others fought for his honor with the ardor and enthusiasm of a Roman soldier. Seldom are the members of the Ethics class so exercised over a question brought before them as they were over the discussion of the ethics of the life of the late Jay Gould. At the beginning of the discussion the feeling of the class was largely adverse to the career of Mr. Gould, but at the end of the argument the sentiment of the debaters bore more evenly upon the scale of criticism. The subject, as presented to the class, read : " Does the career of the late Jay Gould deserve public approbation ?" The attack was led by a young man who spoke as follows:

"Jay Gould, as Napoleon, was the outcome of anarchy. His grinding, griping, and grasping business methods were devoid of honorable or honorable elements. Their adoption inflicted great loss and injury upon every class of society, and there was little in his career deserving of public approbation. He was the leader of the founders of trusts and monopolies, against which our government is legislating. An honorable business man, in whom reside worthy and noble elements, who loves virtue, truth and honesty more than money, is a true citizen and deserves the esteem of his community. Not so with Jay Gould who ignored the common welfare and followed the maxim : 'The end justifies the means.' He created nothing but unscrupulously appropriated what others had created ; he was a law breaker—opposed to government. 'Mr. Gould was respon-

sible for the greatest financial disasters that occurred in modern times. Resulting from this was an increase in crime—business was paralyzed, vast industries stopped, thousands of men and women being thrown out of employment and left without means of support. Many were forced to steal their bread. The influence which such millionaires exert over young men is exceedingly dangerous. Young men seeing the political and social advantage—the power and influence which wealth purchases—are enticed away from worthy employments and become fortune hunters in the hazardous forest of speculation. The shores of life are littered with the wreck of ruined speculators. He who was the cause of inflicting such deep and lasting injury by his example—who was the direct cause of much poverty, misery and crime, should have left some of his immense accumulations to institutions of charity and reform. But no; not a cent to church, charity or education did he leave. All of his miserly savings were left to be guarded by his family."

The next speaker, in support of Mr. Gould, gave quite a complete history of the gentleman from the humble beginning of the poor farmer's boy, to his achievement of the titles "Railroad Magnate" and "Wizard of Wall Street." "Mr. Gould," he said, "by dint of unwavering perseverance and arduous application to business on the ladder of domestic, social prosperity, until he became the common system of railroads, has long connects this country from the Atlantic to the Pacific. While he was not perfect—no man he—and may have committed some acts which deserve not public approbation, I believe his endeavor was to do right by his fellow-men. This gentleman has been unjustly accused of many things. One of the greatest charges brought against him is that he was responsible for that catastrophe known as "Black Friday." Mr. Gould was little more to blame for this financial collapse than any other rich speculator. This panic involved the business foundations of the world—was universal in London, Paris, Berlin, Vienna, and other countries as well as in the United States. It would be the height of folly to charge this dreadful occurrence to any one man, were he ten times as rich and powerful as the late Jay Gould. That Mr. Gould took advantage of this crisis to increase his own wealth is true—who would not do the same? He had a perfect right to do so. It was his extraordinary shrewdness, sagacity, and foresight that served him here as it did all through life. Had the men of this country who are continually crying "down with the capitalist," and claiming fraud, only half the sagacity shown by this great financier, and would they apply it to their own business, they would be more successful in life, make better citizens, and would not have so much time to be finding fault with other people. Mr. Gould, by lending his immense capital to many enterprises and corporations, not only increased his fortune, but made possible the employment and support of 300,000 men and their families. Two hundred thousand happy homes to-day bear witness to his genius. Where then is the ground for complaint? This man, who has been so slandered, never hesitated to do a charitable act for the worthy: no case of real distress ever came to his notice that he did not offer immediate relief. He did not hide his faults from the world, nor did he parade his good qualities and advertise himself as a public benefactor. He was kind and gentle to the weak and needy, but terrible to his rich and powerful antagonists. His domestic relations were the happiest. Living a plain and unostentatious life, he was adored by his family whose slightest wish was law to him, and in the quiet circle of his fireside he ever found the greatest happiness and rest from the toils and cares of his busy life. Jay Gould, to me, appeared as a glorious picture of a self-made American citizen."

" Hard work," the next man said, " can be viewed from different standpoints. I give Mr. Gould credit for being a hard worker, but the tend-

(Continued on eighth page.)

FIGURE 2

An 1893 copy of the *Summary* of Elmira, New York, Reformatory. (From the files of the Library of Congress.)

"flavor" of periodicals we have read, it is well to state, by way of warning, that any one sending improper matter, or contributions the thought of which is not their own, is liable to find himself in an unpleasant position. We want no borrowed ideas.[4]

Although no records are available concerning the financing and sponsorship of the *Summary,* its content would support the conclusion that it was the first internal penal publication produced as part of the institution's operation. There were no ads; subscriptions were sold for $1.00 annually through the institution; and changes in editors were made by the prison's administration.

Our Paper and the Prison Mirror

Little is known about the early days of *Our Paper,* a small periodical emanating from the Massachusetts Correctional Institution at Concord in 1885. Only one sample copy has been retained by the Library of Congress, Number 9 of Volume 8 (1893).[5] Content of that issue followed along the lines of Elmira's *Summary,* and may have been influenced by it (Figure 3).

The *Prison Mirror* (Figure 4) of the Minnesota State Prison at Stillwater, the first penal newspaper in the western areas of the country, came into existence on August 10, 1887.[6] With the full encouragement of Warden H. G. Stordock, fifteen convicts contributed a total capital of $200 to get the paper underway. Among the fifteen shareholders were three famous bad men of the "Wild West," the Younger brothers of the Jesse James gang;[7] Coleman and James Younger provided $20.00 each, Robert only $10.00.

4. The *Summary,* January 1, 1893, p. 8.
5. Queries about files of early years to the institution, regional historical societies, and public libraries did not uncover any other copies. *Our Paper* is still being published as a bright little 9½ x 13-inch bulletin-type monthly from handset type, with the assertion that it is the oldest continually published penal periodical.
6. Fortunately, the Minnesota Historical Society has a complete file of the *Prison Mirror.*
7. Cole was best known of the brothers. He was a guerilla officer in the Civil War. The fact that his father was murdered in Missouri by a band of northern sympathizers was used to justify the life of crime he and his brothers followed. Cole and three of his brothers joined with Jesse James shortly

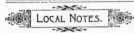

LOCAL NOTES.

—Snow.

—Present this morning 951.

—A blizzard from blizzardville.

—Last consecutive number 5372.

—Arrivals this week thirteen; departures twelve.

—Library books must not be taken to the dining room.

—It thundered and lightened Monday night. Also it snowed.

—Winter displays a very vigorous condition for a broken-backed old fellow.

—The grades this morning are as follows: First, 358; second, 546; third, 47.

—Of the last hundred men received, but twenty-five per cent were misdemeanants.

—The plumbing class benches have been rearranged, affording more room to set up work, etc.

—Commissioner Lee of the Columbian Fair Commission paid the Reformatory a flying visit on Friday.

—Winter's snow and March wind were harnessed together on Monday and made a "rip-tearing" team.

—The blacksmith class is about to begin the regular blacksmith drawing course, having completed the preliminary course.

—The amount of snow in the yard is prodigious. Teams began its removal from the most used portion of the grounds today.

—The storm of Wednesday effectually blotted out from the landscape the course of the Assabet for a time, producing one wide waste of snow.

—Library books *must not* be written in or marked in any manner. Any one doing so will not only be reported, but may also lose the privilege of the library.

—Monday was universally conceded to be the roughest day for out-door work that we have had thus far this winter. And it was none too easy a job keeping warm indoors.

—The class in bricklaying have just built a section of cornice such as will be used on the extension of the east wing. The result is satisfactory, and shows the class capable of very good work.

—Hon. Richard Olney of Boston who has been selected by President-elect Cleveland as Attorney General in his Cabinet, was a classmate of Chaplain Batt of this Reformatory, at Brown University.

—Tonsilitis, bronchitis, laryngitis, influenza, asthma, sciatica, pneumonia, rheumatism, la grippe and lumbago, "cricks in the back" and "stitches" in both sides, are among our present afflictions.

—Passengers on the early train to Boston from Concord and other places were obliged to walk from Stony Brook to Roberts on account of the smash-up on that section of the road last Saturday morning.

—There are at this time eight men in the Reformatory who have been examined by the Commissioners for release and are being held for further test, or as they themselves would say "have got set-backs."

—F. B. Munroe, real estate agent, has recently sold for Frank Jewett about 14 acres of land between the Junction and Westvale, to James Lawler of Westvale, who intends to dispose of it in house lots at an early date.

—The following committees have been chosen to forward the building of the new church, by the society: On building, Messrs. Scott, Wright, Wood, Hodgman and Campbell; on plans, Messrs. Hurt, Elmes, Damon, Batt and Campbell.

—The Sloyd classes have been suspended for a few days, and the benches thoroughly overhauled. Work was resumed yesterday. A few boys have nearly finished the Sloyd course, and show good careful work in all their models.

—Owing to the severity of the storm it was impossible to procure fish for Friday's dinner, and the inmates were obliged to struggle along with oyster stew. They stood it manfully, however, and we have heard neither complaint nor sigh of regret on account of the variation in the bill of fare.

—The regular school examinations took place on the 23d and 24th instants, except in classes A and B. A class will be examined in the Chapel next Wednesday evening, and B class in schoolroom No. 2 on the same evening. As soon as percentages are made up, promotions will be made, which will probably number from fifty to fifty-five.

—Mr. Norris' "bird's-eye" view of Concord Junction and vicinity is ready for delivery. Officers and Instructors who have subscribed for this picture, and intend to have it framed, cannot do better than to have the frame made by the carpentry class who have done some very excellent work of that kind lately. Send in your requisition early.

—About eighty per cent. of all inmates committed to the Reformatory are assigned for school instruction. Since the last school examinations there have been 143 commitments to the Reformatory, of whom twenty-nine were excused from school attendance for various reasons. Of the balance, forty-two were assigned to the primary classes, forty-nine to the intermediate classes and twenty-three to the advanced classes.

—Well, we are in it. Very much so. We haven't lost our grippe. On the contrary we have a grippe which is both tenacious and numerous. On Monday the hospital count began to grow. On that day it increased from 17 to 23; on Tuesday to 32; on Wednesday to 50; on Thursday to 58; and on Friday to 82, of whom 30 are in the convalescent annex. The increase is due wholly to the influenza, or grippe. Fortunately the type is comparatively mild, and there are no indications of anything but good recoveries.

—The later commitments to the Reformatory have been of a high general average, so far as intelligence and physical condition are concerned. If this can be held to mean that there is a more general knowledge and understanding of the intent and scope of the Reformatory it is a matter for congratulation. There have been a few notable exceptions to this, however, one instance being that of a man who had served on three sentences, twenty-four out of the last twenty-seven months in other institutions; another, that of a man partially demented. Of course it is to be expected that there will be great differences among the men in a place like this. We noted the other day a quartette consisting of a broker, a doctor, a journalist and an artist; and another consisting of four tramps. To such differences as these there can be no objection, provided all are justly committed, but if the broker had served a term or two in State prison and the tramp was half crazy, there would be serious objections which ought to be readily seen by any one.

—Owing to the terrible weather of Washington's Birthday, the liberty of the yard could not be given, as is usual on holidays. Breakfast was at the usual time, and from the dining hall the men marched to the shops where they spent the morning in such ways of amusement as circumstances and surroundings permitted. The scenes in the different shops were animated and cheerful. Impromptu concerts, wrestling matches etc., all

with the utmost good order and good nature made the time pass quickly un til ten o'clock, when the men marched to their rooms, changed their shoes, completed their toilets and then (10.30) marched to the chapel for the entertainment.

The entertainment was by Prof. Mohr, prestidigitateur, ventriloquist, cartoonist and lecturer. As a "one man show" the Professor is a howling success. His prestidigitation was good, consisting of the ordinary egg, silver, card and disappearance tricks, all of which were done with elegance and ease. The ventriloquism was clearly the best we have ever listened to, the climax being reached when Prof. Mohr played a zither accompaniment to a ventriloquial comic song, sung clearly and distinctly with a silver dollar between his teeth. The cartoons were exceedingly graphic, the series showing the changes which come to a young intelligent clean-cut face by upward or downward courses of life being especially so. The Professor in the course of his entertainment drew an outline portrait of a fine looking young man whom he met in western Massachusetts last fall, now prosperous and successful, whom he first met at the Reformatory as an inmate four years ago. Some of the officers recognized the portrait, also one or two of the men, but there were few here then who are with us now.

The men marched from the chapel to the dining hall for dinner, thence to their rooms where they passed the remainder of the day. Notwithstanding the inclement weather there were quite a number of visitors to friends and relatives.

Her Husband's Tribute to Mrs. Hayes.

(From a recent interview in the Philadelphia *Inquirer*):

"She was, I believe, one of the most wonderful women the world has ever known," said the ex-President. "She could do more things than any woman I ever met, and she did them all well. She had a most beautiful soul, and she was the personification of love. She was thoroughly in sympathy with the world, and she was always doing some kindness for those about her.

"During the war she was the angel of many a camp, and she was loved by the soldiers and by everyone. She had more power over others than any person I have ever known. I remember an instance that occurred when she was a girl. A boy had crushed his hand, and he was in such terrible pain that he went into spasms when the doctor attempted to dress it. They could do nothing with him, until at last someone suggested sending for Mrs. Hayes. She came, and she at once quieted the injured boy, and inspired him with confidence in the doctor, and he allowed his hand to be dressed. The next day the same scene occurred, and it was feared that the results would be serious, until at last the boy said: 'I think if you would send for Auntie Hayes I could let the doctor touch my hand.' This was done, and the hand was dressed without trouble.

"There is a picture of Martha Washington in the White House. It hangs, you know, just next to that of Washington on the east wall of the East Room. Many people now suppose it was always hung there, it fits so naturally to that of Washington, but Mrs. Hayes was the one who placed it there."

FIGURE 3

The local page of an 1893 edition of *Our Paper* of the Massachusetts Correctional Institution at Concord. Except for the reprint in the lower right corner, the page is filled with short items about the institution and its inmates. (From the files of the Library of Congress.)

The Prison Mirror.

Vol. 1. No. 1.   Stillwater, Minn. Wednesday, Aug, 10th, 1887.   Price 5 Cts.

OUR MOTTO: — — — "GOD HELPS THOSE WHO HELP THEMSELVES."

PRISON OFFICIALS.

—:: Inspectors, ::—

E. G. BUTTS, ... Stillwater.
JOHN F. NORRISH, ... Hastings.
LIBERTY HALL, ... Glencoe.

—:: Resident Officers, ::—

H. G. STORDOCK, ... Warden.
J. A. WESTBY, ... Deputy Warden.
JOHN COVER, ... As't. Dep'ty. W'd'n.
FRANK BERRY, ... Clerk.
H. E. BENNER, ... Steward.
W. H. PRATT, ... Physician.
F. H. HALL, ... Hospital Steward.
GEORGE P. DODD, ... Storekeeper.
W. J. MATHEWS, . . Protestant Chaplain.
M. E. MURPHY, ... Catholic Chaplain.
MRS. SARAH McNEAL, ... Matron.

SALUTATORY.

"The Prison Mirror" casts its first reflections upon the world.

And sheds a ray of light upon the lives of those behind the bars.

Its Founders, Its Mission, And Its Management.

STATISTICS OF POPULATION.

Of The Minnesota State Prison For The fiscal year ending July 31st. 1887.

To the Public.

We Wish He Was Rich.

Contributions.

FIGURE 4

The first issue of the Stillwater, Minnesota, *Prison Mirror*. Among the founders listed at the top of the third column are the Younger brothers of the Jesse James gang. (From the files of the Minnesota Historical Society.)

The first issue of the *Mirror* listed only one editorial staff member, editor Lew P. Schoonmaker, but the masthead also named two compositors and the "printer's devil": Cole Younger. The listing of the outlaw probably was a gesture of recognition arising from the bandit leader's fame. A printer's devil—a shop clean-up boy—was not a position meriting mention in the masthead.

Aside from the glamor of some of its founders, the *Mirror* is especially interesting because of its vitality, its advanced aims, and its unusual method of original financing. All these are shown, to some degree, in the paper's salutatory message, reprinted here, verbatim and in its entirety:

SALUTATORY

"The Prison Mirror" casts its first
reflections upon the world.

_____

And sheds a ray of light upon the
lives of those behind the bars

_____

Its Founders, Its Mission,
And Its Management

It is with no little pride and pleasure that we present to you, kind reader, this our initiatiave number of THE PRISON MIR-ROR, believing as we do, that the introduction of the printing press into the great penal institutions of our land, is the first important step taken toward solving the great problem of true prison reform. With this our maiden issue, of the Mirror is born a new innovation into the heretofore dark, dreary, monotonous existence of those whom fate hath led downward to the narrow confines of a prison cell and branded as social outcasts; upon the darkened lives of such, it shall be the one great mission of THE MIRROR *to reflect a glad ray of hope to light and encourage them*

_____

after the Civil War to form one of the most daring outlaw bands of the West. They were especially known for robbing banks and trains, and it was during the robbery of the bank in Northfield, Minn., on September 7, 1876, that Cole and his brothers were caught and sent to the Stillwater prison. Two townspersons were killed during the holdup, and the brothers were given life sentences. Robert died in prison in 1889, but Cole and James were paroled in 1901.

upward toward a higher and nobler life, to banish from their hearts the midnight gloom of prejudice, envy and malice, and in their bosoms reflect the cheering light of reason, truth and love.

It shall be the untiring mission of the MIRROR *to encourage prison literary talent* and *to instruct, assist, encourage, and entertain all those within our midst,* and *to scatter words of warning upon the unwary pathway of those in the outside world, whose reckless footsteps may be leading them hitherward.* In thus sending forth to the world this humble little sheet, we trust and pray that it is destined to become the corner stone of the great pedestal whereon shall stand the living statue of truth, bearing aloft the flaming torch of mercy, justice and reason; and from the sands of this tiny booklet there may be gathered many brilliant gems of truth to forever decorate the sovereign heads of honor, manhood and right. It shall be our earnest endeavor to bury meloncholy, estrangement, and enmity in the vast region of the past, and to sow in the hearts of our readers the golden seeds of charity, hope and love.

This, we believe, is the only printed sheet now in existence, organized, published, edited and sent forth to the world by prisoners, confined within the walls of a penitentiary.

In thus extending to us the privelege of publishing and sending forth to the world THE PRISON MIRROR, our Warden, Mr. H. G. Stordock, has, we feel, extended to us a most elevating and beneficial privelege, which we trust, will be most fully appreciated and honored by each and every prisoner within our midst.

The great success which has thus far attended our little enterprize has already been far in excess of the most lofty dream of its founders: which fact we owe to the great kindness, encouragement, and assistance of Warden Stordock, Deputy Warden Jacob Wesby, Ass't Deptuty Warden John Cover, and our "rustling" outside business manager and treasurer, Mr. Geo. P. Dodd, Prison Store Keeper, and to the officers of the prison, in general, to whom, one and all, we return our most earnest thanks and deepest gratitude. We also appreciate most highly, the many kind words of encouragement which has been extended toward us by the "boys."

THE PRISON MIRROR will be issued on Wednesday of each week, and will contain continuous contributions upon all general subjects, sketches, words of wisdom, jokes, poetry, etc. from the pens of our comrads in prison: also a general budget of prison

news, and possibilities, and realities, never before offered to the
public: *also a general report of the financial condition of the
prison:* prison statistics, etc. *of interest and value to the taxpayers
of the State,* the public, and the fireside: it will contain each week,
words of warning to the young from the pens of those who know
whereof they speak, in verification of that great scriptural truth
"the way of the transgressor is hard." THE MIRROR will be moral
in tone, instructive, and entertaining, and should find a place in
every home, and at every fireside: *its management will be without
official interference, and soley in charge of the managing editor,*
who will use his every endeavor *to maintain it a credit to the
"boys," and an honor to the Warden.* . . .

Our exchanges will be distributed gratuously to the inmates of
this institution: which feature of our enterprise, will alone, be
most highly appreciated by our unfortunate fellowmen, inasmuch
as they will thus be provided with an unceasing flow of pure,
fresh, entertaining and instructive literature, thus keeping them
educated and informed with the steady advance and progress of
the great outside world, and thus be prepared, when the hour of
the restoration to freedom shall dawn, to meet the glad era, upon
an equal footing with the world, and we trust, regain and maintain
the position of honorable, upright men and useful citizens; and we
feel and trust that the great press of America, and especially of
Minnesota will not permit us to want for exchanges to fulfill this
part of our mission.

In thus sending forth our tiny sheet to our mothers, fathers,
sisters, homes and friends, and the world at large, we present
thereto a model gem of minature literature, born and sustained
under difficulties, but which we are fain to say will prove a boon
and a blessing to our brethern in prison, our homes and humanity,
believing, as is indicated by the motto of THE MIRROR that "God
helps those who help themselves."

With the above remarks by way of introduction, and most
earnestly soliciting the kindly assistance and support of our readers, we most humbly submit to their kindly encouragement, the
future success of THE PRISON MIRROR.[8] [Italics added.]

8. Editor Schoonmaker's salutatory message occupied most of page 1,
Volume I. Incorporated in it was the following "Agreement of the shareholders
of the *Prison Mirror*":
"We the undersigned do hereby voluntarily loan to the 'trust fund' for the

Its redundancies, poor spelling and punctuation, and other mechanical lapses notwithstanding, Editor Schoonmaker's salutatory contained objectives for a penal publication so complete and commendable that they withstand critical evaluation even eighty years later. The italicized portions of the message pinpoint these objectives; they could serve equally well as guideposts for penal publications in the late 1960's. Note that, even at such an early date, the *Mirror* was launched with the editor "solely responsible," without official interference, for its management. The middleman role of the editor, with the necessity of satisfying both the convicts and the warden, was understood by Schoonmaker.

A letter from Warden Stordock accompanied Schoonmaker's announcement. In it he said:

> The PRISON MIRROR is now before you. If it shall prove a
> failure then the blame must all rest on me. If it shall be a success
> then all the credit must be given to the boys who have done all the
> work. It was necessary to have my consent before the experiment
> could be tried, and therefore I am responsible for the venture. I
> hope and believe that a generous public will give the MIRROR all
> the encouragement that it shall deserve, and as it does not cost the

purpose of starting a prison paper, under the management of Lew. P. Schoonmaker, the following sums opposite our respective names, said sums to be replaced to our several credits with interest thereon, at the rate of three per cent per month, from the first earnings of said paper, and when full amount of said loan with due interest thereon is so refunded and paid to our private accounts in the prison office, our claims upon the stock, material, and shares of said paper shall cease, and said stock, material and shares of said paper, become the property of the prison library, and a part and parcel thereof: and the net profits of said paper shall be devoted exclusively to the prison library, in the purchase of such books and periodicals as the Warden may select; and we hereby pray that you will accept this, and consider the same an order to pay the said respective sums opposite our names, to the treasurer of said paper, Mr. Geo. P. Dodd, and charge the same to our several accounts."

The agreement was signed by Schoonmaker, the Younger brothers, and eleven other convicts. Schoonmaker, Cole Younger, and James Younger each contributed $20; Robert Younger was on the list for only $10. So far as can be determined, no other prison publication has been launched with funds derived from inmate shareholders. The fact that the most famous convicts in the prison, the Younger brothers, were among the founders must certainly have helped the paper gain quick acceptance among its inmate readers.

> State anything and only the prison library can be benefited, the
> people will, I feel sure, bid it "God-Speed." The one feature of
> the MIRROR that ought to be of value to all tax payers will be the
> financial statement of the receipts and expenditures of the
> prison. . . .
>
> If the local papers will reproduce from the MIRROR, every tax
> payer in Minnesota can at the end of the year know just as much
> about the management of the prison as the officers of the institu-
> tion. This prison belongs to the people and they have a right to
> know how their money is expended. . . ."

In other items originating from the warden, it was obvious that he felt
strongly that the *Mirror* should perform an external information role,
especially by making regular public accountings of the funds of the
prison.

The laudatory objectives with which the *Mirror* was launched
formed the basis for an excellent prison newspaper, far ahead of its
day. Content was "homey" and interesting, as well as informative. The
sense of humor of its editor was evident, too. Here are some representative local items verbatim from the first issue:

> All the newspapers throughout the country are very profuse in
> inviting President Cleveland to pay a visit . . . THE MIRROR, not
> to be outdone in courtesy extends a like invitation in behalf of its
> "retired community." We will not send, however, a committee to
> convey our invitation.
>
> ———————
>
> Receiver E. S. Brown paid us $10.00 for the first printed copy
> of THE MIRROR.
>
> ———————
>
> The stone steps leading into the new main cell building is a
> great improvement.
>
> ———————
>
> The prisoners will do well to observe closely the rules governing
> the prison library, which will appear in our next issue.
>
> ———————
>
> The editorial eye of THE MIRROR has peeped into several "resi-
> dences" on the top ranges, which were not in as neet and cleanly

condition as might be; come "boys" brace up, and don't furnish us with any more items of this character.

Nearly one thousand volumes of new books, comprising works of the most eminent and favorite authors, have been added to the Prison Library during the past week, to accomplish which Warden Stordock advanced as a loan to the library fund from his private purse, $250.

The "boys" occupying quarters opposite THE MIRROR office are delighted with the window which the Warden has had cut through the four foot walls to admit air and light into their heretofore dark, close and gloomy abodes.

Cole Younger, our genial prison Librarian, has received new honors at the hands of THE MIRROR by being appointed to the honorable position of "printer's devil;" in which position he will in the future keep the flies off the gifts of "wedding cake," and other editorial favors of like nature which may find lodgement in our sanctum sanctorum.

There were scores of other similar human interest items, a couple of more significant items about penology, and an abundance of advertising in the *Mirror*'s first issue. Although, like all prison publications, it has had its ups and downs according to the capability of its editors, the *Prison Mirror* has maintained a generally high level of quality through its lengthy history.

OTHER PENAL PAPERS BEFORE 1900

Only five other present-day penal publications, two of them in juvenile institutions, originated prior to 1900.[9] These are the *Boys'*

9. These publications were still in existence in the late 1960's; it is impossible to know how many others may have been founded only to live a short while. In most penal institutions, then and now, maintenance of files of the institutional publication has not been considered a matter of major importance, and undoubtedly some periodicals were born and died without having their existence recorded.

Messenger, Montana State Industrial School, 1889; the *OPNews,* Ohio Penitentiary, 1892; the *Pendleton Reflector,* Indiana Reformatory, 1896; the *Hawkeye,* Iowa Men's Reformatory, 1898; and the *Mentor,* Massachusetts Correctional Institution at Walpole, 1898.

The longevity of these publications is amazing. To survive through all of the changes in administration and public attitudes required courage and caution, patience and perseverance, of inmate staffs and administrators alike.

These requisite qualities were not always present, and in one particular instance, a penal newspaper brought so much attention and popularity to itself that it was responsible for its own homicide. This was the *Star of Hope,* founded at Sing Sing Prison, Ossining, New York, on April 22, 1899, later published under the names *Star-Bulletin* and *Sing Sing Bulletin.*[10]

Once again, the salutatory of the editor and a message from the warden in the first issue reveal the motivations for the new periodical:

SALUTATORY

"Be to its faults a little blind,
Be to its virtues very kind."

With the timely suggestion that these lines present, we are gratified to be able to lay before the inmates of the institution the initial number of the STAR OF HOPE, thereby augmenting the field of institutional journalism. In extending a salutation to our readers, we realize that one could not occupy an editor's chair under more favorable circumstances. We are relieved of the remorseless pangs of unstable subscription lists or delinquent advertisers. The paper happily has no subscription price, consequently the prospects are fair for a full complement of subscribers, and our treasury will not become depleted by large fees to its contributors. Under such circumstances, we are pleased to announce that the STAR OF HOPE has been brought into existence by the forethought of the Warden and the approval of the Superintendent of Prisons, for the benefit of us *all.*

10. There has been some attempt to link the *Star of Hope* with the *Forlorn Hope,* but aside from the similarity in name, there is no connection. Warden Sage's notice in the first issue of *Star of Hope* clearly indicated that this was the first publication at Sing Sing and that its inaugural had been contemplated for some time.

The paper is ours, and its place in history rests entirely in our hands. Its aim and scope will be to furnish the inmates with a summary of the news of the world, and to stimulate interest among the men toward higher and nobler mental training. The questions of criminology and penology will be liberally presented, and religious and educational interests will always find space in its columns. We solicit your aid and cooperation, invite suggestions and criticism, and ask your kindly consideration of our efforts, and hope that each one may be the recipient of some profit through the paper's existence, and that the efforts put forth by those directly connected with the publication may not be in vain.

—No. 1500

And the warden's message:

NOTICE

The Warden has had in contemplation for a long time the publication of a paper in the institution.

He now proposes to carry his project into effect, and the first number of the STAR OF HOPE is laid before you.

It is contemplated to have the matter of the paper, so far as it is practicable, the product of the pens and minds of the inmates.

This will serve a twofold purpose. Physical labor of the men is, unhappily, to a certain extent restricted at the present time. A fair substitute, perhaps, will be found in the employment of their mental energies.

The effort of composition is real labor sometimes, as many will testify. It will be occupation at least. Again it will conduce to mental training.

All of the inmates of the institution are invited to submit articles. Naturally all cannot be published, but each man will have the benefit of the effort. . . .

—Omar V. Sage, Warden

Other articles in the first issue underlined the necessity for some means of occupying the energies of men in the prison, which apparently was a major factor in Warden Sage's decision to publish the *Star of Hope*. The prison's industries could not accommodate all the men who desired to work, and the paper said hopefully that warm weather might make it possible for men to do some outside work shortly.

From the outset, the *Star of Hope* had an unusually professional air about it. The anonymity of the staff (numbers were used exclusively for identification) permitted no specific knowledge of the personalities involved, but the first editor, Convict 1500, did reveal that he had an especially well-trained staff. In an article in *The Bookman*, he reported that one staff member had held every position from copy boy up to managing editor of a leading New York daily.[11] The paper's cartoonist was a former newspaper artist who had killed his sweetheart. The *Star*'s nameplate (Figure 5), a scenic picture of a star hovering over the prison's wall and guard tower, with the peaceful countryside in the

VOL. I.   SING SING PRISON, SATURDAY, APRIL 22, 1899   NO. 1.

PAROLE LEGISLATION.

WRITTEN FOR THE STAR OF HOPE.

Apart from the question of the immediate punishment of the crime committed, all penal legislation should have a twofold object in view. First, to act as a deterrent against the commission of crime by others, and secondly, to effect the reformation of the individual criminal and his transformation from a lawbreaker to a healthy and useful member of the community at large. Formerly, the first of these objects only was considered as having practical value, and an effort was made, by increasing the rigor of the punishment inflicted, to inspire such a dread of the consequences of crime as to prevent its commission. This theory, that the severity of the punishment would be effectual to act as a preventive, reached its culmination in England in the latter part of the 18th century, when to sheep stealing and murder were meted out the same penalty—death by hanging—and men, women, and even children, were executed by scores for trivial crimes. Experience, however, soon satisfied thoughtful men that the object desired was not to be accomplished in this way. Crime was increasing, and the extension of the death penalty to new offenses, so far from preventing the commission of those crimes, seemed only to augment the number of criminals. It was seen that some new method must be devised to curb the rapidly growing demoralization of all classes, and early in the present century transportation beyond seas was put forward as promising to relieve the congestion of crime in England, and, at the same time, by forced colonization, build up the newly acquired territory in the South seas. This method met with a partial success, and large numbers of criminals were transported to Botany Bay and

than 20 years, but only persons under 30 years of age, who have not been previously convicted of felony, are eligible to be sentenced to that institution, and the act of 1889 was intended to extend it to all classes. At the sessions of the Legislature of 1898 and 1899, laws were introduced, under the sanction of the Statutory Revision Commission, which reënacted the parole provisions of the law of 1889, and, by an amendment to the Penal Code, made it mandatory upon the judges to sentence all persons under an indeterminate sentence. This act failed of passage in 1898, and it is yet undecided whether it will pass or not. During the past winter, Warden Sage submitted to the Governor a bill, which he had carefully prepared, and which embodied the results of his long experience in prison administration, providing for the extension of the parole system as well to those now in confinement as to those hereafter sentenced, and on conferring with the Governor in regard to the matter, the latter, while approving of the principle of parole, recommended that it be not presented during this session, but that the whole matter should be carefully considered during the recess, and an adequate bill be carefully framed before the meeting of the next Legislature, to be presented to it.

It would seem, therefore, that it is probable that at an early date the parole system will be established in this state, applicable to all classes of offenders, either in the form of an indeterminate sentence law, mandatory in requiring the judges to sentence all persons under its provisions, or by a parole law, which would leave the term imposed by the sentence to be fixed as it is now, but would provide that upon the fulfilment of certain conditions, the convict will be entitled to make application to be released on parole. It becomes pertinent, therefore, to the present time to inquire what are the distinguishing features of the parole system, and what results would probably be

DEGENERATE'S REVENGE.

WRITTEN FOR THE STAR OF HOPE.

Even the men who read as they run must be impressed by the constant iteration of our mentors that this is an era of disillusion and innovation. Gradually we have been deprived of our belief in William Tell's archery, the indigestible properties of hard-boiled eggs and all of the cherished and innocuous legends and superstitions that have tended to make life pleasant. This we have endured without audible complaint, believing that the interests of truth and science (which we are told are convertible terms) required at least our acquiescence. Aside from boiling our drinking and washing water and microscopically examining our food before eating, the physical discomforts inflicted upon us have not been great. We have renounced our pet dishes with mental protest, but were somewhat compensated for our renunciation by the knowledge that we were thereby attaining "the higher civilization." Of course, the flesh has mutinied at the command to transform our kitchens into laboratories and have our beloved tyrant, the cook, superseded by a chemist; but we have even contemplated that impending domestic revolution with a far-fetched pride in thinking of the future generations that would be benefited by our self-denial. Those of us who are excessively "carnal-minded," have attempted to avert this culinary "progress," by refering to familiar zoölogical phenomena; for instance, the goat, which begets those which are physically and mentally his equals, yet never judges the degree of decay; but the definition, it is said by our mentors that goats have got "psycho-mentalities," however hardy their digestive organs may be. So, we had become prepared (almost) to thoroughly spiritualize ourselves; to believe that the "Arkansas Traveler," never existed and that his

FIGURE 5

One of the principal features of this first issue of the Sing Sing *Star of Hope* was the ornate nameplate etched by one of the country's most able counterfeiters. (From the files of the New York Public Library.)

11. No. 1500, "Prison Journalism," *The Bookman* (November, 1903), p. 281.

background, was hand engraved in copper by one of the cleverest counterfeiters in the country.

After three months of publication, the *Star of Hope* was enlarged from eight to sixteen pages; its circulation and coverage were expanded to cover convicts in the five New York State prisons. About 5,000 copies were produced biweekly. The editor apparently got excellent support from inmates; about twelve hundred of them contributed items during its first four years. In one month, 311 poems, mainly from the women's prison, were submitted for publication.

The *Star of Hope* began to receive some criticism as early as 1910. At that time sociologist Isabel Barrows commented that the paper displayed a lack of good taste. She thought some of the brevities and jokes were questionable, and did not think that items about races and prize fighting should have been permitted. She also questioned some of the fiction:

> Stories that turn on the hero's making of a fortune by the turn of the roulette wheel so that he can buy his sweetheart some five-thousand-dollar pearls are not very wholesome for the two or three thousand prisoners who read this paper. They rather counteract the otherwise wholesome spirit of the paper and the good advice in the editorial columns.[12]

Real success, and real trouble, came after the paper was combined with the *Mutual Welfare League Bulletin* to become known as the *Star-Bulletin,* and finally, in 1919, as the *Sing Sing Bulletin.* Charles E. Chapin, city editor of the *New York World* and known as "the toughest city editor of all time," had murdered his wife and was confined in Sing Sing Prison. When Lewis E. Lawes became warden, Chapin was in the prison hospital and not expected to live. But Warden Lawes offered Chapin the editorship of the *Bulletin,* and it seemed to provide the necessary incentive for him to overcome his malady. He was out of bed in a week. Chapin, who had fired 108 reporters during his professional career, is supposed to have pushed his prison staff so hard that the warden had to reprimand him, saying, "You know, Chapin, you

12. Isabel C. Barrows, "Periodicals in Prisons and Reformatories," in Charles R. Henderson (ed.), *Correction and Prevention* (New York: Charities Publication Committee, 1910), p. 249.

can not drive these men the way you drove reporters on the *Evening World*. These men are convicts." [13]

Chapin thrived in his work, and so did the *Bulletin*. Outside newspapers saluted his efforts, and the limelight of publicity shone brightly on Chapin, the *Bulletin*, and Sing Sing Prison. Disliking the glare of publicity, New York penal authorities decreed that the publication be discontinued, and Chapin commented that he "made his prison newspaper so popular that it choked to death on its own popularity." [14]

NEW PENAL PUBLICATIONS, 1900–1940

At the turn of the century, a few hardy papers from the eighties were still celebrating birthdays. However, most of the growth in the press at correctional institutions was occurring in juvenile and federal institutions. Pre-World War I foundings included the *Boys' School Herald*, Indiana Boys' School, 1900; the *Echo*, Iowa Training School for Boys, 1904; the *Boys Banner*, Alabama Boys' Industrial School, 1905; the *Uplift*, Stonewall Jackson Training School (North Carolina), 1910. These juvenile publications were followed by two federal magazines, the *Atlantian*, Atlanta (Georgia) U. S. Penitentiary, 1912; and *New Era*, Leavenworth (Kansas) U. S. Penitentiary, 1914; and only one in a state penitentiary, the *Bridge*, Connecticut State Prison, 1915.

Entry of the federal institutions into the publications field with the *Atlantian* and *New Era* brought the penal press one giant step closer to the significant aspect of journalism that it is today. Both publications have developed into magazines of unusual quality and have gained reputations, not only for their deluxe appearance but also for their depth treatment of important crime and punishment topics. Both were evidence that changes in penal administration were on their way.

New Era, for example, was established shortly after a change of administration at Leavenworth and marked the beginning of the decline of the Auburn "silent system" there.[15] Warden Thomas W. Morgan instituted Sunday afternoon yard periods in which men could

13. "Jail Journalism," *Literary Digest*, June 5, 1937, p. 25.
14. *Ibid.*
15. "Leavenworth: The Early Years," *New Era* (Summer, 1964), p. 51.

mingle and talk freely, motion pictures were presented—and *New Era* was introduced on February 27, 1914, as the weekly inmate newspaper. Over the years it has changed from a weekly to a monthly magazine and finally to a slick quarterly.

One of the editors in the twenties was Dr. Frederick A. Cook, the explorer whose claim to discovery of the North Pole in April, 1908, has been a matter of controversy ever since. Dr Cook's seven years in Leavenworth were only a small part of a long, adventurous life.[16]

As a young man, fresh out of New York University Medical College, Cook answered an advertisement seeking a surgeon for an expedition to North Greenland. This resulted in an association with Robert E. Peary, a naval engineer and arctic explorer, that was to bring him world acclaim and then bitter humiliation.

After serving as Peary's surgeon in the 1891 Greenland expedition, Cook returned to the arctic and antarctic areas several times as commander or surgeon of exploring parties. He also attempted unsuccessfully to reach the peak of Mt. McKinley in 1903, then reported attainment of that goal after a second attempt in 1906. Honored as the first to scale America's highest peak, he again turned to arctic exploration. This time he was determined to capture the biggest exploring prize still remaining: discovery of the North Pole. Peary, who had failed in previous attempts to reach the Pole, also organized an expedition at about the same time. Cook's claim of success with his expedition was cabled from a Danish ship on September 1, 1909: "Reached the North Pole April 21, 1908." Five days later came Peary's wire from Labrador, "I have the Pole, April 6, 1909."

At first acclaimed as discoverer of the Pole, Cook eventually lost out in the fight with Peary for official recognition of the feat. The polar controversy was fierce and bitter. Before it subsided, Cook had not only lost the battle for official recognition of his polar claims; his conquest of Mt. McKinley was also discredited.

His conviction for fraudulent use of the mails in 1923 and the subsequent confinement at Leavenworth brought further humiliation. After expeditions to India and Borneo, Dr. Cook had been asked to serve as an oil geologist in Wyoming. Promotional material mailed

16. Russell Gibbons, *Frederick Albert Cook* (Hamburg, New York: Dr. Frederick A. Cook Society, 1965).

while he was forming a company to develop Wyoming oil lands brought on the conviction and a fourteen-year sentence.

The explorer's prison record was about as remarkable as his pre-confinement background. Rather than react with the bitterness that imprisonment so frequently evokes, Dr. Cook put his talents to many uses. He was in charge of the night shift of the prison hospital for a time and also served as superintendent of the institution's night school. He engaged in medical research in the field of drug addiction; and he edited the *New Era* almost single-handedly from 1926 to 1930.

The *New Era* under Dr. Cook's editorship was published as a newspaper until it was converted to a 6 x 9 inch magazine in March, 1928. Rarely was any of the content provided by other authors. A note in most issues advised readers that all articles were the work of the editor unless otherwise credited, and there were very few by-lines. Dr. Cook gave the *New Era* audience reading fare that was amazingly varied and interesting. Stories of Borneo explorations, articles giving practical medical and sanitation advice to inmates, and inspirational essays were combined with occasional news items and poetry to provide a remarkable potpourri of editorial offerings. A cheery, optimistic tone always prevailed.

Although Dr. Cook and his friends continued to fight for his polar discovery claims while he was in prison, he did not use the *New Era* to advocate his cause. In only one available issue, April, 1927, was the subject discussed. Colonel Charles M. Forbes, a former veterans administration official serving time in Leavenworth, favorably reviewed Dr. Cook's record in that issue (Figure 6).

Dr. Cook, whose application for probation in 1927 was granted and then reversed, was released after serving only seven years of his sentence. He spent his declining years lecturing and fighting for recognition. He was awarded a full pardon by President Franklin D. Roosevelt on May 16, 1940, just three months before his death.

Only a few penal publications came into existence in the roaring twenties. The *Messenger* of South Dakota Penitentiary was founded in 1921; the *New Leaf* of Green Hill School, Washington, in 1922; the *Island Lantern* of the Federal Penitentiary on McNeil Island, Washington, in 1924; the *Criterion* of the Ohio Reformatory at Mansfield in 1927; the *Hill Top News* of the Michigan Reformatory at Ionia and

Published Every Month
at the
**UNITED STATES
PENITENTIARY**
LEAVENWORTH
KANSAS
With the Permission of the
Department of Justice

LEAVENWORTH
NEW ERA

For the Encouragement and Educational Advancement of Prisoners Everywhere

Edited by Prisoners
NON-SECTARIAN
NON-POLITICAL
Distributed only to
Persons Especially Interested in
Prison Reform
and to
Government Officials

VOLUME XIV   LEAVENWORTH, KANSAS, APRIL, 1927   NUMBER 111

Validity of The Polar Claims

An Unbiased Review of the Facts

BY COL. CHARLES R. FORBES

I HAD just finished reading Will Durant's story of philosophy, and on my small table there rested several other interesting volumes, among them Galahad, and Emil Ludwig's recent biography of Napoleon, and several books dealing with polar expeditions. I had read so much of the controversy as to who climbed the pole first, that I decided to read the polar stories next.

There were the newspaper accounts of Amundsen's achievement, Commander Byrd's flight, and the books setting forth the claims of Peary and Cook. After reading these narratives with their records of discovery, it occured to me that I might write something for the benefit of our readers first, because two of the noted explorers whose names appear as experts in these writings, had been my commanding officers—Admiral W. S. Schley, U. S. Navy, and Major-General A. W. Greely, Chief Signal Officer, U. S. Army.

What Experts Have Said and Are Saying

Both of these men had themselves spent prolonged periods in the Arctic, and were considered as authorities on the subject.

I have had a good deal of time here to review and study and concentrate—and the problem of polar discovery has greatly interested me and only as above indicated but because a large part of the public regards it as an unsolved mystery, with published records before me. I regarded it as my duty to endeavor to analyze and compare and classify the facts that enter the claims in polar discovery.

No advocate of the controversy can afford to ignore the important comment made and published over Admiral Schley's signature at the time when the polar agitation was a throbbing issue —Schley said: "Either both have been to the pole, or he who came second copied the first." And General Greely was quoted as saying recently that "Cook's proofs were as good as Peary's," and it is further reported that Captain Sverdrup and most of the European explorers are of the same opinion today.

I have never taken any active side in the polar controversy, but I believe the facts as they come to me through my personal acquaintance with several explorers speak for themselves, and I cannot understand how the stories that were circulated during the heat of the controversy have become so firmly settled in the minds of the public as facts.

How Can Polar Attainment Be Proven?

The question arises, how can we prove the validity of the claims of a polar traveler? There is no tribunal, or society or other organization of any kind who could properly assume the authority to pass upon such claims. It appears to me that the correct and only judgment is the slow process of mass opinion of later generations. The work of all explorers has been thus rated. As the original reports of the discovery are digested and assimilated, and as later explorers verify or discredit the earlier records, an explorer's work takes its permanent place in the pages of history. The rival polar claims must take a similar course.

The position taken by Rear Admiral Schley, backed as it is and as nearly all of the Arctic explorers is still the only outline of a system by which the polar claims must be tested. This system embodies a careful comparative study of the records of polar explorers, and from this angle, the remarkable reports of both Byrd and Amundsen would seem to close the argument.

All Later Explorer's Verify the First

It is claimed that four expositions have reached the North Pole. If so, the reports should affirm or deny each other. From this angle, let us examine the records of polar endeavor.

It may be remembered that the early theories of conditions at the top of the globe were that the North Pole is in the center of a deep open sea from which the centrifugal motion of the earth had thrown the ice away from the Pole and against the surrounding shores.

(Continued on page three)

The War Mother

BY JOHN SCHLITZ

EDITOR'S NOTE: The following is the sculptor's own story of his statue of The War Mother, which has just been completed in the Stone-Shop.
It is to be presented to the American War Mothers Association. It is to be secured permission from the Department of Justice for Mosher to execute it in marble, and have shipped him a huge block of marble for the purpose.

T HIS motherly figure presented in the model portrays the noble calm of true maternity. Neither haughty nor sorrowful. She expresses the soulful mood of love purest and truest.

Her head is slightly bowed in reverence for the nation's ideals; her patriotism surpasses the anguish of the holocaust she has witnessed.

In her right hand she holds a torch, the true emblem of the fire of love, the flames of ineffable self-immolation. It is the torch of human love and compassion, of liberty and emancipation. Its flames are born of, and led by, blood and tears. Its radiations are those of ideals realized.

On her left stand the fasces, symbolic of united strength, over which stream the Stars and Stripes, softly enfolding her whom we hold dearest and sacred, in whom are centered the ideals of the nation.

Resting gently, her left hand clasps, within a fold of the flag, an olive-branch, the symbol of truce, of understanding and of peace enduring. The remainder of the flag rests softly over her right arm and shoulder, the shoulder upon which reposes the burden heaviest, the arm from which her strength, valour, and virtue emanate. Who among us has not experienced the noble, prudent, loving guidance of Mother's arm?

The corona encircling her head is a modification of the crown of the American War Mothers. The chaplet of oak-leaves bespeaks strength and courage. When the war clouds gathered, lowering over the Nation, was not her's the greatest fortitude?

The back of her chair is graced by a large American Eagle, upon whom she leans for support. His wings spread over the Nation. In their shadow there is rest and peace. He will ever protect his sacred treasure.

The breast of the Eagle is adorned with the American shield; the emblem of safe-guard and of the ideals in which this nation was conceived. The legs of the chair are those of the Eagle powerful. His talons are firmly rooted in the soil of the United States, which forms the relief map, the pedestal whereon the statue rests. Our lofty protector will ever clasp that which is hallowed to him. Fain would he raise it to his own lofty heights. Herein are indicated his office and the ideals of which he is emblematic.

(Continued on page three)

Our Mother

By 24160

How oft some passing word will lend
In visions to recall
Our truest, dearest, fondest friend—
That earliest friend of all.

Who tended us in childish years,
Those years that pass as hours,
When all earth's dewy, trembling tears,
Lie hid within her flowers.

Thou star that shines in the darkest night,
When most we need thy aid,
Nor changes but to beam more bright
When others coldly fade!

Oh, mother! round thy hallowed name
Such blissful memory springs
The heart in all but years the same
With reverent worship clings.

Thy voice was first to greet us, when
Bright fortune smiling o'er us,
And thine the hand that's readiest then
To lift the veil before us.

Or if dark clouds close round our head
And care steals o'er the brow
While hope's flowers fall crushed and dead
Unchanged mother still art thou.

The Making and Breaking of Human Races

Future Will Call For Special Breeds of Men, Much as We do For Pedigreed Stock

BY FREDERICK A. COOK, M. D.

N EW races are like young men, they feel the impulse of coming and passing generations—the sunrise of a new life leaves in it it's shadow, the soul of earlier culture, but that earlier culture is the sum total of thousands of years of study and development. Why condemn it with one stroke of the pen as we have done with each succeeding drift of racial and social offspring? There is a distinct breed, with all that goes with the fine pedigree of animal culture in every race of man, but we seem to lose sight of this important problem because civilization as we have it today has been moving to the composite of Egyptian, Greek and Roman rules of life. But Egypt had an advance civilization and this leads us farther back into Asia as the probable source of pre-Bible culture.

Central Asia the Cradle of Human Race

What has become of the successive stages of peoples who had a vigorous civilization in India and China? About has become of the still earlier peoples who roamed over Europe and Asia long before dominating races took this main stage of human endeavor? In each and every race ever developed there was a mental, a physical, social and a political stream worthy of preservation and permanence. The thousands of races whose blood and culture have poured a continuous stream for thousands of years into the life arteries of civilization are all now forgotten, but originally each had a distinct family history, very special attributes, as a vocation in a distinct and special life, and always certain outstanding physical and mental attributes. Some had long noses, some had long heads, some had long legs, some were dwarfs and some were giants. Some were black and some were white, others were yellow and red but all were unique in their own kind and in their day. Modern man is therefore a composite in color of all earlier races but in spite of this known blood admixture we still retain a strong prejudice against color and racial blending.

We see the children of the black and white, we pity them and we call it a bad mixture. We encounter offspring of the Indian and the White and we pronounce the result a calamity, and we abhor the thought of a melting pot for the yellow and the self-styled superior white races, but is this perception of social cultural color and racial admixtures sound?

Influence of Mother Culture

An unbiased study of the prejudice against inter-racial mating soon determines that the good or bad effect of the offspring of a mixed race is mainly the influence of mother culture and the results that we see are mostly the outcome of an unnatural sexual entwinement among the lower racial representatives.

When a trained engineer long on adventure but short on family culture marries a wild woman, the offspring must suffer. In a like manner when a Spanish Adventurer in the tropics marries a negro woman of jungle habits the children start from nowhere and end as a football of fate. Such mismating can have no other results and it is by an observation of these types that we conclude that the yellow or the red people of other races do not mix well with whites. In the present state of civilization it is dangerous to advocate intermarriage among races of different color but the greatest misfits are a result of intermarriage among families of high and low stages of culture. The difference between the highest and lowest development of man is greater than the distance between the mind of man and that of the beast, but in spite of this, mating abortions of this kind are of daily occurence. Therefore if we are to correct the calamity of the miscarriage of matrimony let us begin at home.

(Continued on page two)

FIGURE 6

A copy of *New Era* edited by explorer Frederick A. Cook. The left-hand column contains a defense of Dr. Cook's exploration claims; the right-hand column is by Dr. Cook.

the *Young Citizen* of Arizona State Industrial School for Boys at Ft. Grant, in 1928. The *Island Lantern* was one of the most influential penal publications in the 1930's and still is an excellent literary magazine.

The depression years brought on a significant increase in the establishment of penal publications. Perhaps because the public had other worries than the "coddling of prisoners," more institutions produced magazines "with almost harelike frequency." [17] Some of the more prominent publications started in the thirties are the *Spectator*, Southern Michigan prison, 1930; the *Eagle*, Federal Reformatory for Women at Alderson, West Virginia, 1933; the *Menard Time*, the consistent prize-winner of the Menard Branch of Illinois State Penitentiary, 1934; *Presidio*, Iowa State Penitentiary, 1934; *Hill Top Crier*, Indiana State Farm, 1934; the *Lens*, United States Penitentiary at Lewisburg, Pennsylvania, 1934; *Joliet-Stateville Time*, Illinois State Penitentiary, Joliet-Stateville Branch, 1935; the *Colony*, Massachusetts Correctional Institution, Norfolk, 1935; *Shadows*, Oregon State Penitentiary, 1935; *Weekly Progress*, State House of Correction and Branch Prison at Marquette, Michigan, 1938; *Forum*, Nebraska Penal Complex, 1938; and the *Spokesman*, Georgia State Prison, 1939.

Of this group, the *Menard Time* (Figure 7) stands as the leading example of the excellence that can be achieved by a penal publication when it has the necessary support. It was started in 1934 under the administration of Warden Joseph E. Ragan, who brought John A. File, editor and owner of the Chester (Illinois) *Herald-Tribune*, to the prison staff to teach printing.[18]

At that time only hand-set type was available, and only two pages could be set at a time because of the scarcity of type. A budget of $500 was provided to purchase type and an old hand-fed press. The paper had to be folded and cut by hand; the print shop was only 900 square feet. But it had the most important ingredients for a good start: solid administrative support and a trained professional to guide its develop-

17. Herman K. Spector, "What Men Write in Prison," *Tomorrow* (December, 1945), p. 55.
18. The material on the *Menard Time* that follows is from its thirtieth anniversary issue, February, 1964, and an untitled, undated mimeographed history of the paper, except as noted.

THE Menard TIME

1865 1966
ASSOCIATE MEMBER
ILLINOIS PRESS
ASSOCIATION

ASSOCIATE MEMBER
1966
SO. ILL. EDITORIAL ASSN.

America's Foremost Prison Newspaper
First-place National Winner of 1965-66 American Penal Press Newspaper Contest
Established 1934

VOL. 17, NO. 2   MENARD, ILLINOIS ★·★·MARCH 1, 1966   20 Pages

9 OF 10 WON HONORABLE DISCHARGES

Convict GI proved worth in WW II; Prison returns fell to record low

Illinois convicts released into the Army during World War II violated their paroles four times less than prisoners paroled into civilian life today.

This fact was revealed in a comparison by The Menard Time of a 1960 sociological report on Illinois paroles who fought in WW II and today's national parole violation average.

According to a seven-page sociological treatise researched, compiled and written by the past president of the Illinois Academy of Criminology, only 100 of 2,942 felons paroled to combat in WW II violated their paroles.

Author of the treatise is Hans W. Mattick, research director of the Chicago Youth Development Project. A research sociologist and former guest author for The Time, Mattick offered the article for publication.

19 of 20 Succeeded

The Army parolees violated parole 5.2 per cent, the article said, compared with Illinois' civilian violation of 22.6. Today's national average is 25 per cent.

Other facts brought out by Mattick:

—That a similar program during WWI was officially termed a "distinct success."

—A follow-up study eight years after the end of WW II showed that the Army parolees compiled a recidivism (return to prison) rate of one-sixth of those who finished prison sentences and did not fight.

—That homicide and sex cases —both of which have the lowest violation rates—were not accepted by screening boards.

Records Were Unknown

—That 84 per cent of the Army parolees served their country without their military superiors knowing of their past records.

—That 75 per cent of the parolees were promoted, compared

Turn to Page 2

3 of 4 Menard prisoners say 'I'll fight Viet Cong'

Three of very four Menard prisoners would battle the Viet Cong if paroled into the Armed Forces, a Menard Time poll of more than 825 inmates has shown.

Although Selective Service regulations restrict acceptance of parolees into the Armed Forces, a study of almost 3,000 Illinois paroles who fought in World War II has revealed that only one in 20 later violated his parole.

The cell-to-cell canvass, conducted by the Menard Time's editorial staff, asked this question: "Would you fight the Viet Cong if paroled into the Armed Forces?"

• Answers showed:

—That 72 per cent, or 596, said they would fight if given the opportunity.

—That 24 per cent, or 199, said they would not.

—And that 4 per cent, or 30, said they were of "no opinion" or had "no comment."

A similar three-day poll of 180 Minnesota State Reformatory prisoners showed that 78 per cent said they would fight and that 22 per cent had refused.

Patriotism Sweeps Prisons

Since January, convicts in Texas, Wyoming, Nebraska and Illinois have petitioned State or Federal officials to fight. Prisoners at Montgomery, Ala., State Prison donated 242 pints of blood for wounded GI's in Viet Nam.

Illinois convicts would be considered for parole into the Armed Forces if the Selective service System changed their regulations, but State officials are helpless until then.

In an official statement of policy of the Illinois Parole and Pardon Board, Supt. Francis R. Barron answered a Menard inmate's inquiry.

Barron's letters said in part: ". . . please be advised that when the regulations of the United States Selective Service System and the Armed Forces permit paroled inmates convicted of felonies to serve in the various branches of the Armed Forces,

Turn to Page 2

VIET NAM

U.S.

CONVICTS

Menard Time Drawing

FIGHTING VIETS 'AIN'T SAFE'

Fighting Viet Cong "just ain't safe," is the reason one man declined to accept parole into the Armed Forces if it were possible.

His candid comment was one of many transcribed during a cell-to-cell poll conducted here recently when men were asked: "Would you fight the Viet Cong if paroled into the Armed Services?"

Prisoners answering 'no' were asked 'why?'

"Because I'm a devout coward," one man said honestly. Other answers?

"Because I'm plain scared— They took all the fight out of me at the court house. . . Because it's against the Geneva charter. . . . Because I'm in one mess now and I'm not gonna jump into another one. . . ."

UNTAPPED MANPOWER

More than 200,000 felons in Federal and State prisons in the United States are possible material for enlistment into the Armed Forces. During WW II nearly 3,000 felons from Illinois prisons were paroled into the Army—only five of every 100 were found in prison years later. Present Selective Service regulations forbid acceptance of ex-convicts.

Use convicts: war hero

———— Story, photo--see page 5

FIGURE 7

The *Menard Time,* monthly newspaper of the Illinois State Penitentiary, Menard Branch, is professional in appearance as well as in content.

ment. Improved physical facilities came later as the paper made its reputation as one of the better members of the penal press.

During its more than thirty years of existence, the *Time* changed its format three times, and was published as a magazine for a while. At its inception it was a three-column, eight-page paper only 8 x 10 inches in size, edited and written mainly by the prison chaplain. The paper was soon turned over to inmates, but was under strict censorship. From 1941 to 1943 it was published as a magazine, then was suspended for six years.

With its reissue in 1949, the *Time* became a tabloid-size newspaper produced from machine-set type on a new cylinder press. Improved equipment and working conditions brought results. Circulation went from 1,500 in 1949 to 1,800 in 1952, and 2,500 in 1954. By 1965, more than 7,500 copies were being circulated in the fifty states and twenty-six foreign countries. Its greatest success has come since 1952, at which time it was again suspended and faced a very real crisis. Riots shook the Menard institution in 1952, and some correctional authorities said the newspaper was instrumental in the riots and urged its removal. Publication was stopped by Warden Jerome Munie, but it was resumed shortly thereafter when Governor William G. Stratton appointed a new administrator for the troubled prison.

Governor Stratton's appointee was Ross V. Randolph, later director of Illinois' Department of Public Safety, whose background then included positions as supervisor for the Federal Bureau of Investigation, administrative assistant to Governor Adlai Stevenson, and high-school principal. A *Menard Time* writer tells of the new warden's actions with the newspaper:

> "The Menard Time" was one of the targets of the new and vigorous warden. He came to the print shop . . . and called the staff together. He talked to them as men.
> "You men have an opportunity to accept the responsibility of being real newspapermen and putting out a paper that can help the men in this institution help themselves," he said.[19]

Warden Randolph gave the *Time* his support, named David Saunders, who had been feature editor, to edit the rejuvenated newspaper,

19. *Menard Time*, December 25, 1964, p. 7.

and it was on its way to an exalted position. Saunders, who had been sentenced to forty years for murder as an eighteen-year-old in 1950, was the first of several editors to make good with the paper and with their own lives. While Saunders was editor, Governor Stratton proclaimed a "Menard Time Day" throughout Illinois in the paper's honor. President Dwight Eisenhower sent a congratulatory message in 1959 for the *Time*'s twenty-fifth anniversary, saying, "I heartily agree that . . . [the *Time*] . . . can contribute much to the spirit and effectiveness of Menard." The Illinois Press Association and the Southern Illinois Editorial Association extended associate membership to the *Time*. In July, 1960, Dean I. W. Cole of the Medill School of Journalism and Chairman John E. Stempel of the Indiana University Department of Journalism named the *Time* as the nation's best prison monthly. Circulation expanded, especially outside the prison.

For David Saunders, personal success reached its most important milestone in 1960 when Governor Stratton commuted his sentence to thirty-three years. He was paroled in July, 1961, after eleven years at Menard, to take a job on the Troy (Illinois) *Tribune,* and one month later was made editor of the *Carterville Herald*. He has since resigned to earn a journalism degree at Southern Illinois University where he has been employed in the Public Information Office.

Under Saunders and the editors who followed him, the *Menard Time* has made many contributions to penal journalism and to its prison community, as well as to penology in general. A *Time* story on the value of prison barber schools led to the reversal of a ruling in New York which prevented ex-convicts from having barber licenses. An editorial campaign for amending the Illinois parole law led to a change in 1961.[20] Worthwhile projects such as the March of Dimes,

20. State Senator Paul Simon explained the *Time*'s role thusly: "The Menard Time played a very real part in the bill which I introduced in the 1961 session and which became law. It was through an article in the Menard Time that I became aware of the discrepancy in service given to those who were paroled and those who were discharged. . . . I learned that the prisoner who has a job on the outside and who has relatives and friends waiting to help him is given parole and supervisory assistance. The prisoner who has no job on the outside and no friends or relatives to help him serves his full time and is discharged with $25 and a suit of clothes and left out in the cold. In reality, as the Menard Time pointed out to me, the one who is discharged needs the help more than the one who is paroled. As a result of this I

Blood Banks, and the like, have been especially successful at Menard because of the *Time*'s campaigning. Material it has compiled has been used in other states to fight for the abolition of the death penalty.

Credit for the *Menard Time*'s success is shared by many: prison administrators, inmate editors, officials of state government, and college professors. Warden Ragan's appointment of John File, an experienced news man, to the prison staff, and the selection of Herbert Gerdemann, a journalism school graduate and a newspaper publisher, to carry on after Mr. File's retirement have been major factors in the newspaper's continued success. And a "first" in prison education, the teaching of a college journalism class inside Menard's walls by Professor Charles Clayton of Southern Illinois University, contributed to the professional skill of the staff. All in all, the combined efforts of many have made the *Menard Time* a model penal newspaper since its debut in 1934.

THE MODERN PERIOD, 1940–66

Despite the longevity of several penal publications, the penal press is basically a development of recent years. As Figure 8 shows, the large majority of them have been founded since 1940. In fact, more than one-half were started since 1950, and more than one-fourth since 1960.

The excellence of prison publications like the *Menard Time, New Era, Atlantian, Prison Mirror* and others, has obviously helped the penal press win acceptance and grow. But modern developments in prison administration undoubtedly also have been responsible for a greater use of periodicals in correctional institutions. Increased attention to rehabilitation rather than punishment, an awakened understanding of the importance of communication in any society, and

---

introduced a conditional release program where most prisoners now receive a 90-day parole period prior to actual discharge date. The result has been a savings of perhaps $400,000 a biennium in actual cost, as supervisory care is considerably less costly than custodial. In addition, the program has been eminently successful and there is evidence that indicates we have reduced the number of prisoners who return to prison almost automatically, for most of those who go wrong again do so during this 90-day period." (Letter from Senator Simon, October 31, 1966.)

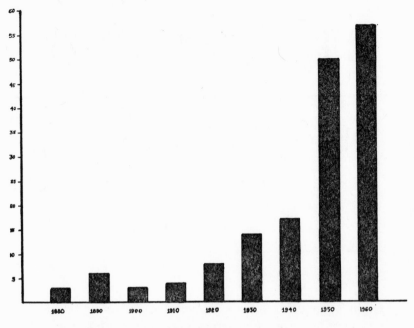

FIGURE 8

This bar graph shows the number of prison periodicals founded in each decade since 1880, plus the partial period 1960–66. Note that more than half the prison publications reporting a founding date were started between 1950 and 1966.

increased freedom and responsibility have served to make prison publications the rule rather than the exception.

Their rapid growth in the last few years would seem to indicate that prison publications will become even more common in the very near future; perhaps as common as employee magazines in companies or newspapers on the college campus. Scarcely any corporate organizations or educational institutions are without printed communication media now. Prison publications have earned their present position through efforts in the past; with increased attention to their goals— their basic role in a penal society—they should achieve still greater respect and use. Increased effectiveness of the penal press plus changes in penology could very well make it an unusual prison that will not have a magazine or newspaper.

CHAPTER 3

Objectives of the Penal Press

You can't organize a riot or dig a tunnel while beating hell out of a typewriter or watching to make sure that a printing press doesn't gobble up the whole stack of paper in one gulp.—Al Nussbaum, "The Penal Press," NEW ERA, Summer, 1965.

THE CRYPTIC ANALYSIS above was not far from a goal for the penal press in its earlier days. In many instances, prison publications were founded out of a warden's desperate search for constructive activity for his charges.[1] Prisons were overcrowded; work assignments were not plentiful enough to go around; anything to break the idleness that bred discontent was worth a try. Many meritorious achievements have come about in strange ways, and one should not be too critical of the

1. See Warden Omar V. Sage's notice of publication of *Star of Hope* on page 35.

48

cause, so long as the effects are laudable. Unfortunately, for too many penal publications and for too long a time, the effects too closely resembled the cause. Notable exceptions are pointed out in the previous chapter, but many early efforts of penal publications reflected no real concept of the constructive goals available to them. They were only "busy work" and showed it.

Significant advances in the worth of the penal press have come with the years, but considerable soul-searching is still being done to seek out the most important areas for concentration. Leadership in this search actually has come from the convict editors themselves, but prison administrators and outsiders have also contributed. Views from all quarters as to the goals of the penal press will be presented in this chapter, along with some conclusions derived from these opinions.

THE ADMINISTRATOR'S VIEW

No matter how you look at it, the penal press could not exist without the sanction of prison administrators. And perhaps the most amazing thing about the penal press is that wardens permit it to exist. More than 20 per cent of the questionnaire respondents reported that their publications had caused administrative problems; approximately 11 per cent said they have had problems serious enough to discontinue the publication or reclassify the editor as a result. Newspapers and magazines will always be potentially troublesome in the prison situation, so the penal press has been and will continue to be on trial as far as prison administrators are concerned. If prison publications fail to measure up to the expectations of the administrator, they may be killed off or, at a minimum, flounder hopelessly because of lack of material support.

Administrators ordinarily are, by nature, pragmatists. Charged with the responsibility of maintaining a secure and orderly society of convicts, their emphasis naturally tends to gravitate toward the pressing problems of shelter, food, clothing, and discipline. It is to their credit, however, that most of them work hard to improve rehabilitation programs and to satisfy the needs of their residents for mental and spiritual recreation. But all programs must prove their worth; manpower and facilities are not available for ineffective programs.

The fact that a little more than half of the U. S. penal institutions have publications indicates that the penal press has passed the test in the majority of cases, but there is a sizable minority yet to be persuaded. Just what do wardens and their associates think the penal press is doing or should do? What is the test to be passed? For answers to these questions we shall have to rely on officials at institutions with publications, but it seems reasonable to assume that most officials at the non-publication institutions would disagree.[2]

Wardens or publications supervisors at the institutions with publications were asked to check which of the following seven objectives their publications tried to achieve. They were also requested to list any others. Following are the objectives and the number of responses tabulated for each:

1. To provide an outlet for creativity   147
2. To improve morale of inmates   128
3. To give inmates a constructive way to spend their
   time   88
4. To provide journalistic training   83
5. To give officials a means of communication with inmates   73
6. To give officials and inmates an opportunity to make
   the public aware of penology problems   73
7. To provide vocational printing training   53
8. Other objectives   22

The three objectives most often cited form a rather strange mixture. The second two—to improve morale and to give a constructive way to spend time—are in line with the practical approach that would be expected; each is directly related to the main problem of maintaining discipline and preventing disorder. But the first one, "to provide an outlet for creativity," is an intangible that one might not expect from "hard-headed" administrators. Judging from the manner in which this

2. This assumption is basically, but not entirely, correct. In most penal institutions where there is no publication the lack is because the administration does not believe in the effectiveness of the penal press. There are, however, some institutions with only short-termers and no need for a periodical, and others in which inmate interest has failed to support a publication.

objective was often expressed on questionnaires and in interviews, it seemed that it was, for many officials, a matter of rote memory rather than serious thought. It seemed to be "the thing to say" about penal publications, but other than that, there was no indication that its real worth had been analyzed. In some instances where this objective was most quickly quoted, the publication was a newspaper that would not accept poetry and fiction. Some officials, however, apparently have expended the effort to consider what this really means (see Chapter 5).

To get some measure of the effectiveness of the publication in accomplishing its goals, the administrators who sponsored publications were also asked, "Have there been any instances in which the publication has been a special help for the administration?" Responses were overwhelmingly favorable: more than 75 per cent indicated that their publications had been a help. Numerous specific examples of this assistance were cited by the administrators.[3] Publications were lauded

3. Typical of the responses are these: "Yes, in providing information concerning board meetings, parolees, etc.," the *Reporter*, Draper Correctional Center, Elmore, Ala.; "Yes, in maintaining morale, disseminating to inmates information from administration," *San Quentin News*; "It has given the administration an opportunity to know the inmates' feelings on many matters, which has proven fruitful," *Soundings*, Maryland Correctional Institution for Women, Jessup; "In two areas, interpersonal relations and public relations," the *Beacon*, Massachusetts Correctional Institution, Bridgewater; "Clears up misunderstandings," *Rocketeer*, Missouri Training Center for Men, Moberly; "Brought recognition by outside newspapers, other sources, as to programs in operation in our institution," *Buccaneer*, Lebanon Correctional Institution, Lebanon, Ohio; "Warden has the opportunity to tell of new ideas, and the where and why for such happenings," *Broadcaster*, Tennessee State Penitentiary, Nashville; "The Texas Department of Corrections is spread over a large area. We have thirteen units situated in an area with a diameter of 150 miles. The paper affords us an easy method of bringing routine matters to the attention of inmates of our units," the *Echo*, Department of Corrections, Texas; "We feel that the publication is a constant source of help. Not only does it keep the majority of our inmate population in a keenly interested state, but it serves as a definite medium of communication between administration and the inmate body," the *Roller*, Bland Correctional Farm, Bland, Va.; "There are times when the magazine has assisted the institution in clarifying policies to the inmate population, gaining cooperation of the inmate body relative to certain features, and served as an organ to disseminate general information," the *Atlantian*; "A publication of New Era's type always reflects favorably on the administration. It is a public relations tool for both the inmates and officials . . . ," *New Era*, Leavenworth, Kans.; "In getting ac-

as an aid in maintaining morale, in providing information about institution programs to inmates, in gaining acceptance for these programs, in improving public relations of the institution, in serving as a means for communicating inmate attitudes to the administration, and in clearing up misunderstandings. In all, sixty-six administrators took the time to elaborate on the special instances of assistance from inmate publications in the administration of their institutions.

To find out how beneficial they thought publications work was for inmate staffs, the administrators were asked, "Do you think publications work has any special rehabilitative effect for the inmates who have major staff positions on the publications?" Again response was overwhelmingly affirmative; 89.5 per cent said it did. There was a remarkable amount of agreement among these respondents, with 60 per cent praising publications work as having a constructive effect on the thinking of staff members and developing a sense of responsibility.[4] Other rehabilitative benefits cited were the use of publications work as a vocational training device (26 per cent) and as an outlet for creative expression (13 per cent). The *Menard Time* reported the successes of two of its former editors as outside journalists following their release; the *Pendleton Reflector* of the Indiana Reformatory reported that

ceptance of programs such as blood bank, information from administrative voices, official advice," *T.I. News*, Federal Correctional Institution, Terminal Island, Calif.

4. Typical comments include: "Above all it teaches responsibility," *Dopester*, Avon Park Correctional Institution, Fla.; "I believe it gives them an incentive to try to set an example for the other inmates, and by so doing they tend to change their way of thinking," *Stretch*, Kansas State Penitentiary; "It encourages creative and constructive thinking, teaches them how to accept responsibility," *Soundings*, Maryland Correctional Institution for Women, Jessup; "It takes them out of themselves and makes them aware of the wider scope of things," *Hill Top News*, Ionia reformatory, Mich.; "It restores, in some measure, their self-respect," the *Prism*, State Correctional Institution at Muncy, Pa.; "Many times influenced by the close contact with superiors and by the selection and editing of material which attempts to understand and evaluate law offenders. Frequently promotes better self evaluation and emphasizes value of social conformity," *Lewisburg Lens*, United States Penitentiary, Lewisburg, Pa.; "We believe it is an excellent self-disciplining activity. We also have found that it does much to improve one's communication skills," *Barometer*, Federal Correctional Institution, Ashland, Ky.; "It is a form of discipline and thought influence," *T. I. News*, Federal Correctional Institution, Terminal Island, Calif.

several former staff members were now working on major newspapers; and the *Reformatory Pillar* of the Minnesota State Reformatory for Men at St. Cloud indicated that "at least 50 per cent of our editors have gone into either a graphic arts or a journalistic field." Others indicated similar measures of success for publication "alumni" in publications-related work, but there was one notable exception. Two out of the three previous editors of the *OPNews* were back in the Ohio Penitentiary at the time this study was made.

In general, however, responses from prison administrators point to some rather definite conclusions. In spite of the fact that penal publications can and do cause problems, those who have used them in their institutions believe their advantages outweigh the problems. They consider the major benefits of these publications to lie in their use: (1) as a medium for internal communication; (2) as a public relations device; (3) as a means for bringing about a greater sense of responsibility and more constructive thinking in the inmate staffs; (4) as a vocational training aid for printing and journalism; and (5) as an outlet for creative expression.

THE VIEWS OF CONVICT EDITORS

Al Nussbaum's quotation at the beginning of this chapter was part of an article analyzing the penal press. Placed in its proper context here, it, along with other inmate-authored comments, shows that many inmate writers have applied their constructive thinking to the role of the penal press:

> Originally, penal publications came into being because they would perform useful functions: They would provide on-the-job training for would-be writers, and they would provide one more way to keep men occupied. You can't organize a riot or dig a tunnel while beating hell out of a typewriter or watching to make sure that a printing press doesn't gobble up the whole stack of paper in one gulp. These were the practical considerations.
>
> Today, the penal press has another goal: It speaks FOR the prisoner, *not* TO him. The primary audience is *outside* the walls where all worth-while changes must originate. The penal press

speaks to lessen the misunderstandings that abound *outside* prison. Penal publications are sent to legislators, politicians, city and college libraries, judges, clergymen, social workers, penologists, doctors, psychiatrists, educators and the editors of Free World magazines and newspapers and the publishers of books. Families of inmates and other interested individuals also receive copies of penal publications. . . .

But the first two reasons for the existence of the penal press are still valid ones: An active man is *not* fomenting disorder, and it *does* spark creativity inside the walls. . . .[5]

Writer Nussbaum, who is confined in a federal institution and works with a slick quarterly magazine, is not alone in his view that reaching the outside public has become the major goal of the penal press. Ed Mello, editor of the *Mentor,* a newspaper serving the Massachusetts Correctional Institution at South Walpole, is convinced that the same change has occurred. Musing about the meaning of the title of his newspaper, he wrote:

Mentor was a character in Homer's Odyssey, and, after the role of this epic character, the word mentor now designates a person, usually an older person, who teaches and counsels a younger, less experienced one about life and the world.

So The Mentor, as we are sure everyone will agree, is a misnomer. For The Mentor is not written to the inmates behind these walls; it is written to the outside reading public—or at least to that part of it that we can reach. And although we are, unfortunately, in a position to inform our outside readers on certain aspects of a specific, limited reality: to wit, penology—we are none of us here in a position to play Mentor to the public. . . .

The Mentor, like so many other things in this world, owes the fact of its present existence to its capacity for a change; that it has been able to change not just its outward appearance from time to time, but also to change its very function when the old one became obsolete or proved itself to be impracticable.

The function it was originally planned The Mentor would perform was as an outlet for the pent-up feelings and frustrations of prisoners. The theory being that if these things were given an

5. Al Nussbaum, "The Penal Press," *New Era* (Summer, 1965), p. 48.

outlet, which was acceptable, that they would not seek some other less acceptable one.

But this didn't work. It didn't work because it was never allowed to. For the prisoners whose pent-up feelings were such that they were not just a personal problem, but also a social one—these men all had and have a deep-rooted sense of hostility and alienation. But if the administration-censor of a penal newspaper has one iron-clad rule, it is that nothing "negative" shall be allowed.

So the original intended function of The Mentor, it soon became evident, was never going to be more than a theoretical one. But if it were not allowed to become a vehicle of expression, then why not at least become a vehicle of communication?

This second choice . . . gradually became accepted. And so The Mentor, with its present personality, came into being.

It is a paper published by and for the inmates of this prison, but written to the outside world. It is our editorial goal to create in as large a segment of the public mind . . . as possible, a true understanding of the realities and the problems—of prison and of being a prisoner. . . ." [6]

A similar opinion appeared in an editorial of *Sagebrush*, monthly magazine of the Nevada State Prison. Editor George Beebe, in his first opinion piece as editor, said:

I can only hope that the most important aim and function of this publication will continue to be realized, i.e., the public will become more fully aware of the human feelings and needs of the men behind these walls. That we all have feelings is sometimes forgotten when the gate slams shut, and that this institution has many pressing needs that must be taken care of soon is not too widely known.[7]

Belief that there is a need to tell their story to the outside public is deep-seated among prison editors. The desire to communicate with outsiders permeates the salutatory messages of editors and most of their reflective articles concerning the purposes for their publications' existence. This desire is coupled with a related goal, as expressed by the editor of the *Forum* of the Nebraska Penal and Correctional

6. "About the Mentor," the *Mentor* (March, 1964), p. 2.
7. "Editorial," *Sagebrush*, VIII, Edition 12, p. 3.

Complex: "It will also attempt to point out the needs of prisoners as they make the transition between imprisonment and freedom." [8] Problems of the parolee, the ex-convict who must overcome the disadvantage of a prison record to succeed in the free world and avoid becoming a recidivism statistic, are considered to be important fare for the pages of the penal press.

There seems to be very little disagreement among penal editors about the goals of their publications. Most of them would agree to the same overall list, but there is variation as to areas of emphasis. Differences in institutions, differences in personalities of the inmate staffs and the administrations, differences in publication format and other dissimilarities of individual situations obviously help account for some of these variations. For example, a somewhat different emphasis stemming from a basically similar philosophy is present with the *Insider,* a monthly magazine of the District of Columbia jail. A formal statement of purpose appears in the masthead: "to afford the inmates an opportunity for self-expression, . . . to serve as a medium for the discussion of public topics . . . to provide an incentive for reformation, and inspiration." In explaining his approach to the magazine, the editor wrote:

> The INSIDER supposedly represents all inmates of the District of Columbia Jail, a typical large institution serving a large and highly populated metropolitan area.
>
> The jail population is made up of males, females, juveniles, elderly prisoners, recidivists, and first offenders, all charged with everything from first degree murder to such horrible crimes as running a red light in violation of the D. C. Traffic Code.
>
> Coverage of news from this heterogeneous population is not always easy. Fortunately the administration permits a liberal policy in the editing of the magazine, the criterion being generally that we stick to facts that can be substantiated, articles that are neither libelous or defamatory, and fiction that may be either dramatic or humorous as long as it is not obscene.
>
> The staff of the INSIDER is not a fulltime . . . crew. Rather it is made up of inmates who do the work in their spare time when their regular daily assignments are completed.
>
> All this description of the prison magazine's function and oper-

8. "Happy Birthday," the *Forum,* May 22, 1965, p. 2.

ation is presented in the way of an introduction to explaining the real reason for such a publication. . . .

A large prison is a community. It contains humor, tragedy, drama and a peculiar culture of its own. And communication is a vital part of any community, inside or outside the walls. Like newspapers and magazines in any community, the INSIDER tries to present the news and portray community activities. It tries to show the humorous as well as the tragic side of jail life. Its writers and editors have tried to do this, in varying degrees, since June, 1947, when the first issue was printed.

Hence the vital importance of the INSIDER, and the penal press in general, is that it provides a few laughs in an atmosphere where laughs are not common. It gets news into maximum security cell blocks into which even pigeons and sparrows find entrance difficult. It presents to readers outside the D. C. jail a literary picture of what life in jail is really like. And it provides its writers an opportunity to exercise a degree of creative expression. . . .[9]

Frequency of publication has an influence on the objectives of the individual prison publication, too. Quarterlies tend to stress creative writing and depth material; weeklies can do more with news presentation. Typical objectives of a weekly are those of the *OPNews*, Ohio Penitentiary:

Since the first issue seventy-three years ago, the editorial policy of the "News" has not changed greatly: To gain benefits for the inmates, to create a friendlier atmosphere in the institution, to keep the civilian population informed of the routine of prison life, and to improve public relations. However, the primary purpose of the inmate staff is to keep the prison population informed of current events.[10]

Again, the statement of purpose for the *OPNews* shows that there is very little difference in the total goal of individual penal papers, nor is there any real difference between the views of convict editors and prison administrators. The differences that do exist are variations in emphasis, rather than in their ultimate ends.

9. "Sounding Off," the *Insider*, D. C. Jail (September, 1965), pp. 4–5.
10. "It's Our Birthday," *OPNews*, April 17, 1965, p. 1.

PROBLEMS AND STANDARDS OF PRACTICE

Prison editors must, of necessity, be concerned with some of the practicalities involved in the day-to-day effort of accomplishing their aims. Most important of these are the uncomfortable "middleman" position they find themselves in, between the inmate population and the prison administration; the need for standards of practice that will prevent activity detrimental to their aims; and some means of unifying their editorial voices with those of similar institutions so they may have a combined strength equal to their tasks.

The inmate population and the administration both draw editorial fire because of their tendency to squeeze editors into a "can't win" position. The *Vaca Valley Star,* California Medical Facility, complained:

> An editor of an inmate newspaper can have his back to no wall and his face to no goal. He can only revolve on his own axis, from censor, to reporter, to copy, to deadline. He orbits without progress because he must operate in a field of journalism which seems ordained to be placed squarely in the middle between the inmate body and the administration.[11]

The editor of the *MP News* of the Montana State Prison directed his main barrage at his peers:

> Unfortunately, the newspaper must first surmount a major obstacle before it can be expected to accomplish its true purpose, and that is the conflict of ideas by the inmate population as to what a prison newspaper should really do. . . .

> Reduced to essentials, it seems to be an either-or proposition—either the prison newspaper attacks the administration or it is against the inmates.[12]

Complaints about the other side of the fence, the administration, are legion and do not require repetition here. It is a rare prison newspaper editor who does not feel that he could do a better job if the administration were not so restrictive.

11. Reprinted in the *Eye Opener* (April, 1964), p. 5.
12. Joe Lucas, "The Iron Voice," *MP News* (November, 1963), p. 8.

Other penal papers come in for criticism on occasion also. A fear is often expressed that, because of an unreasonable approach or unethical standards, other editors may undo previous accomplishments. Editor Eddie David Cox of *Stretch* magazine, Kansas state prison, expressed this feeling well when he said: "The Penal Press is an organization of prison periodicals dedicated to a common cause. . . . No one of these papers can achieve this purpose alone, but when one publication resorts to fiery editorials and exploiting of petty grievances and personal animosities, that publication hurts every prisoner, no matter where he may be incarcerated." [13] He went on to say that one publication alone cannot be very effective in winning the battle, "but one alone can destroy much of what the others have fought so hard to build up." [14]

Plagiarism is a major sin for any writer, and prison editors have been especially sensitive about it because it does rear its ugly head habitually on the penal press circuit. On one occasion the editor of the *San Quentin News* suggested sarcastically that there should be at least one restriction:

> It takes a little something away from whatever reputation penal newspapers may have established over the years when certain authors, probably more out of frustration than intent, publish stories under their by-lines which, in simple terms, they didn't write.
>
> The most glaring example to date was the word-for-word reproduction in a prison magazine of a nationally syndicated columnist's definition of maturity. In the editor's note it was pointed out that this was the inmate's "first piece" for the magazine, and that a "second article" would follow soon. We wondered if this second one might not be "Gone With The Wind," or "Yes, Virginia."
>
> What can we do about it? Nothing. Except maybe suggest that if we must pirate articles to break into print, let's at least steal from each other.[15]

Many inmate editors have attempted to organize formally the penal publications of the United States in order to adopt standards of prac-

13. "Editorial," *Stretch* (June, 1965), p. 6.
14. *Ibid.*
15. Reprinted in *Menard Time*, June 1, 1965, p. 8.

tice and to gain strength through union. Ed Mello of the *Mentor* planned such an organization, "including a sort of wire service, and criteria for being a member," [16] but he abandoned the project as "too involved" for a prison editor. Others have come to the same conclusion, but an amazing semblance of an organization has resulted nonetheless. Although it has no formal structure, the Penal Press (PP) has been accomplishing a great deal as an organization. Any publication from within a penal institution automatically becomes—and remains—a member simply by indicating that it has accepted membership. It is understood, though there is no formal pledge, that certain standards and obligations will be observed by PP members. A mutual exchange of publications and the right of reprinting from other members, provided credit is given, seem to be major benefits of membership.

Almost every editor in the organization has, at one time or another, listed what he thought the ethical standards of the organization are or should be. The most persistent attempt to standardize seemed to come in late 1963 and early 1964. At that time staff members of the *Lake Shore Outlook*, Michigan City, Indiana, set forth a credo and proposed purposes for the Penal Press.[17] Other publications reprinted the purposes as follows:

PROPOSED PURPOSES OF A PENAL PRESS ASSOCIATION

1. To establish co-operation and encourage good relations among the various penal publications in the United States of America.
2. To elevate the quality of journalism in the Penal Press.
3. To encourage ethical, moral, and truthful journalism in the Penal Press.
4. To further the exchange of ideas, information and discussion concerning problems peculiar to inmates of penal institutions relative to their welfare, rehabilitation, or correction.
5. To provide educational stimulation to inmates of penal institutions by means of the Penal Press.

16. Personal letter to the author, March 26, 1966.
17. Reprinted in *Green Mountain Graphic*, Vermont State Prison (February, 1964), pp. 4, 24.

6. To encourage high quality in the literary efforts of inmates of penal institutions.
7. To discourage plagiarism, irresponsible criticism, and bad taste in the Penal Press.
8. To serve as a link between inmates of penal institutions and those members of society at large concerned with their welfare while inmates, and after their return to society.
9. To alert public opinion in society at large to problems incident to and affecting inmates of penal institutions.
10. To promote understanding between inmates of penal institutions and the general public.
11. And generally to focus the efforts of all member penal publications toward the achievement of wholesome and enlightened penology and correction for the rehabilitation of inmates of penal institutions.

No formal action was taken on this, or any other such proposal, and perhaps penal editors will continue to make them for years to come. The editors of the *Lake Shore Outlook,* however, have contributed a good set of standards for the Penal Press that will do, perhaps, until another comes along.

Convict editors are also concerned with the problem of the "tone" of their publications. How can wrongs be corrected without giving the impression of being habitual gripers? How can reasonable sympathy be engendered without the impression of too much self-pity? How can the good side of prisoners be shown without seeming to be engaged in ridiculous bragging? The growth of the belief that the outside public should be influenced by the penal press has made this problem acute. Now not only must an inmate population that is eager for action, and an administration, sensitive to its image, be mollified—but the prejudices of outside readers must be considered, too. That convict editors are aware of their need for restraint can be seen by the following two discussions of the problem. First, Editor Jim Kelly of the *Spectator,* Southern Michigan prison, speaks:

You Cry Alone

The prison newspaper is often accused of being careless in its duty to the men it represents because it does not publish all their grievances. That may be a strong charge and then, again, it may not. The trouble is that a steady publishing of grievances may appear to the reader to be just crying. . . .

In prison, little things have a tendency to magnify themselves in importance until they become immense in our own eyes, whereas, when seen by another, they seem quite insignificant. Our problem, then, is to try to distinguish between those things which are of real importance to the inmate body and those which only appear important to a few individuals, but which are really nothing but "crying.". . .

There are many wrongs which need to be corrected in prison. But the prison newspaper which stresses those wrongs—which continually gripes about them—is not really serving those whose cause it claims to aid. It is committing greater evil by "crying.". . .[18]

Martin Snyder, editor of Leavenworth's *New Era*, expressed his resolution to avoid "tonal" pitfalls in this fashion:

Like an oil portrait, a prison cell or a poem, a penal publication is shaped as much by what is left out as by what manages to get in. To begin with you've probably read a thousand wet-eyed stories about inmates already. We mean every time you pick up any outside magazine or newspaper there's some creepy article about them written by a social worker with a smug attitude, or a tower guard with a chip on his shoulder, or an ex-inmate who had a nagging mother and a lousy alcoholic father and a sister who was a you-know-what. . . . The truth about prison life won't take you into a slick palatable fantasyland of Noble Savages or elegant gonifs with hearts as big as Alaska. Forget about that Disneyland stuff—those ideas are strung together like sausage links; just when you think they should end, along comes another piece of baloney. . . . New Era will take you on a word and picture trip which accumulates the incidents, sights, smells, thoughts, sensitive buttons and short circuits that are the material of prison life—and we will try to do this without the usual slobbery and self-pity, and with only a minimum of hypocrisy.[19]

18. The *Spectator*, May 14, 1965, p. 2.
19. "Editor's Page," *New Era* (Summer, 1964), p. 1.

SOME OTHER VIEWS ON PENAL PRESS GOALS

Some outsiders—that is, some people not incarcerated or connected directly with administering a penal institution—have been sufficiently interested in the penal press to give some thought to its potential. These range from leading educators in the field of penology to merely interested citizens. Whoever they may be, their views, if they come before the prison editors, are given quick attention, publication, and discussion.

Howard B. Gill, Director of the Institute of Correctional Administration at American University, was superintendent of the Massachusetts Correctional Institution at Norfolk between 1927 and 1934, and has been an advocate of a "Community Prison" concept.[20] Thus he speaks as a former administrator, an educator, and a proponent of a prison concept that gives inmates greater participation in the activities of a penal institution. Mr. Gill has said:

> To the extent that the penal press will express both the convict's point of view (uncensored) and that of official personnel on subjects of concern to both, I believe its potential for usefulness in the future is of great significance. Anything which increases communication between prisoners and prison workers is of prime importance. In this connection, I suggest that editorial staffs of prison journals shall consist of both prisoners and prison officials so that both points of view will be presented.[21]

20. Mr. Gill has listed four basic essentials of a Community Prison: (1) Normalcy—as it has to do with inter-personal relationships between officials and staff, with the nature of structures in the institution, with all institutional activities, with rules and regulations, and with the general climate of the institution; (2) Small Group Principle—as this applies to living quarters, dining, bathing, work program; leisure time activities including hobbies, athletics, entertainment, visiting, religious services, and medical care; (3) Inmate Participation—based on joint responsibility for all institution activities except discipline, parole, finances, and similar official administrative actions; and (4) Community Contacts—including bringing the outside community into the prison and taking the inmate to the outside community in all reasonable ways possible. (Described in "What Is a Community Prison," the *Colony*, March 15, 1966, pp. 6–9.)

21. Personal letter to the author, May 31, 1966. Similar views were also

He also made the following interesting suggestion: "I believe it would be worthwhile if the *American Journal of Correction* or *Crime and Delinquency* would publish in each issue comments from or references to significant articles from the penal press so that all correctional workers would have the benefit of such opinions." In his view, the penal press has published too much "chit-chat" and not enough substantial material in the past; but occasional articles have been contributions to penological literature.

Florence Randall, Ph.D., in articles published in several penal publications, has emphasized the duty of the penal press to reach the outside public. She said:

> The penal press has a vital need to reach the outside. In a broad sense prison administrators are appointed to their jobs to carry out the will and philosophy of the whole people in respect to the management and handling of the more than 220,000 human beings in their charge. The people need know something about these inmates. They are not only one's fellow mortals but are also often one's relatives or friends, and easily could be oneself.[22]

Mystery writer Erle Stanley Gardner has also contributed suggestions about the role of the penal press. He too has placed considerable importance on the outside circulation of penal papers. In his words,

> The way for inmates to meet the public is through the prison press. When inmates write stories showing their yearnings, their longings, their ambitions, their recognition of individual problems which caused them to be imprisoned, people will say, "Why doggone it, that fellow is a human being just like I am. His problems are a little more intense than mine, but when you come right down to it, they're the same sort of problems I face in my own life." If we can build up an "outside" circulation for the prison publications as much as possible, and if the inmates can write stories and articles showing their problems as human beings,

---

expressed in a letter to the Editor, the *Interpreter*, Colorado State Penitentiary, Canon City, in which Mr. Gill praised the editor for succeeding in expressing "the convict's point of view as part of a better understanding."

22. Dr. Randall's article, "Possibilities of the Penal Press," made the rounds of the penal press in 1965, but its original publisher was not determined. Most users credited the March 13, 1965, issue of the *OPNews*, but the editor there could not recall from which source he had reprinted.

the results are bound to be for better understanding. And out of that understanding may come intelligent cooperation in the field of inmate rehabilitation. . . . The penal press is far more important than many people think it is.[23]

Further emphasis on the external function of the penal press has come from *Saturday Review* writer James F. Fixx, who has written some of the most knowledgeable material on prison publications to appear in the general magazines. Calling the prison press "one of the most obscure and misunderstood backwaters of American journalism," he observed that, "Read mainly by prisoners, their families, and a handful of other people who for one reason or another take an interest in penology, this corner of the fourth estate is largely unknown to the very audience it is most anxious to reach—the ordinary person with a reasonable concern for the problems of his society." [24]

Charles C. Clayton, Professor of Journalism at Southern Illinois University, was instructor of the first journalism class at Menard prison and the instigator of a national contest for the prison press. As a journalist and teacher he has observed:

> Journalism behind bars . . . has an important therapeutic value inside prison—both for those who work for the paper and those who read it. It makes a definite contribution to rehabilitation, which is, or should be, the primary purpose of any correctional institution. It also contributes to a better understanding of prison and the problems of their inmates by the general public.[25]

From whatever the source—convicts, prison administrators, outsiders knowledgeable in penology, writers, journalists—the expression of legitimate purposes for the penal press is much the same. Emphasis varies, but all who have considered this remote branch of the fourth

23. Original publisher of Mr. Gardner's "The Importance of the Prison Press" was the Nevada State Penitentiary *Sagebrush*, February, 1958. It has been printed and reprinted in scores of penal publications, most recently the June 3, 1966, *Weekly Progress* of the State House of Correction and Branch Prison at Marquette, Mich.

24. James F. Fixx, "Journalists Behind Bars," *Saturday Review*, March 9, 1963, p. 54.

25. "Time Looks to Future," *Menard Time* (February, 1964), p. 4. Also in Charles C. Clayton and David Saunders, "The Penal Press Goes to College," *Collegiate Journalist* (Winter, 1966), pp. 6–7, 13.

estate see basically the same general potential for good. In specific form, the purposes of penal publications could emerge as a long list. Their root goals, however, are three in number: (1) To serve as a communication medium within the prison; (2) to serve as a communication medium between the prison and the outside world; and (3) to serve as an outlet for the creativity of the inmate population.

"Jeepers! No wonder I was uncomfortable last night!"

Bob Matlock, The *Forum* (Nebraska Penal Complex; April 24, 1965), p. 2

CHAPTER 4

Prison Publications as Communication Media

It is a thin line, this line of communication, and over the years it has become more and more well defined until today The San Quentin News *is a positive force in creating an accurate image of the prisoner and prison.*—Cary Johanneson, SAN QUENTIN NEWS, December 9, 1965.

THE ABOVE LINES were written by the prize-winning editor of the *San Quentin News* as part of a story commemorating the twenty-fifth anniversary of his newspaper. In that story he told of predecessors of the *News*, "a four page gossip sheet published in the early Thirties called the *Walled City News* and another four page endeavor called *Sports News*, but nothing that anyone took seriously." Editor Johanneson then went on to say that in 1940, inmates went about the task "of creating an institutional newspaper that would be a force in the lives of the men of San Quentin. More than this they wanted a paper that

67

would also be a force on the outside." In his story about the development of just one prison newspaper, Johanneson was, in effect, outlining the essential change in penal publications in recent years.[1]

Not only the *San Quentin News*, but scores of other penal newspapers have grown from gossip sheets which nobody took seriously into media of communication with substantial potential, both inside and outside prison walls. Recognition of the communication role of the prison press, and its dual internal-external nature has been slow in coming but is now well on its way.

Publication supervisors in institutions all over the country consider their inmate periodicals to be meaningful communication media both inside and outside the institution. At the California State Prison at Folsom, the *Folsom Observer* "offers a medium for explaining new CDC [California Department of Corrections] programs, thereby helping to correct misinformation amongst the inmate body." The *Beacon* of the Georgia Industrial Institution at Alto, in the opinion of its supervisor, "informs families and friends of inmates of the program here and therefore saves the administration the time and effort of explaining the program of the institution to each family individually. Also many influential citizens of the state keep informed on the progress and needs of the institution."

Roger Graham, journalism advisor at the Sierra [California] Conservation Center, reported that the *Nugget* served as a means of communication and of making announcements. "There is a broad breach between the administration and the inmate body," he said, "and the newspaper serves to lessen this breach." At the state correctional institution at Camp Hill, Pennsylvania, the *Headliner* has been of considerable help in "keeping the population informed of institution

1. Cary Johanneson, who also wrote under the name Jon Carey, won first place in the American Penal Press writing contest for 1965. As a writer, he was one of the finest talents among prison editors. In his *San Quentin News* column, "Bastille By The Bay," he sensitively described the emotions and thoughts of the prisoner and vividly transmitted the sights, sounds, and smells of prison life to his outside readers. On August 28, 1966, Cary Johanneson, who was then 27 years old and beginning the ninth year of his life sentence for murder, took his own life. Eloquent tributes by outside writers, who envied his huge talent and sympathized with him for his unfortunate circumstance, indicated that he had, through his writing, proved to some outsiders that prisoners are, after all, human beings.

events and new academic and vocational programs." The *Dan Muse* of the Federal Correctional Institution at Danbury, Connecticut, "has been of great assistance to the administration to define policy, policy changes, and changes of procedures and routines." Supervisors of the *Best Scene* of the Wyoming State Penitentiary at Rawlins and of the *Ad Lib* of the New Jersey Reformatory for Women at Clinton believe that their publications have been helpful in reaching the outside public with information about the programs at their institutions. Scores of others report similar success for their publications. There is a pronounced consensus among the administrators who work directly with inmate publications that they are beneficial for getting information to the convict population and to the public. Emphasis varies, but there is a tendency among supervisors to direct more attention to reaching the inside audience rather than the outside public.

Inmate editors are also enthusiastic about the communication function of their periodicals, but there is a pronounced preference for the outside public as the more important of their audiences. The belief that improvements in penology will come only through public enlightenment has spurred the efforts of editors to reach a larger and more influential outside audience. Editor Ed Mello of the Massachusetts Correctional Institution *Mentor* refers to external efforts as the "larger achievement" for the penal press.[2] Jack Leckey wrote in the *Raiford* [Florida] *Record* that "one of the major functions of the penal press today is to inform the public—society—concerning what goes on within prison walls."[3] Al Nussbaum, in *New Era,* has said, "The primary audience is *outside* the walls where all worth-while changes must originate."[4] Analyzing his primary duty as editor of the *Eastern Echo* of the Pennsylvania State Correctional Institution at Philadelphia, Edward T. Miller decided that it was "to present a compound picture of prison and prisoners to society with a view to promoting better understanding and communication between the two."[5]

Other editors have presented similar views. Along with their increased desire to reach the outside public have come some expressions

2. Personal letter to the author, March 26, 1966.
3. Jack Leckey, "Penal Press," *Raiford Record* (Fall, 1963), p. 30.
4. Al Nussbaum, "The Penal Press," *New Era* (Summer, 1964), p. 48.
5. Edward T. Miller, "Editorial," *Eastern Echo* (Spring, 1964), p. 2.

of disappointment that the number of external readers is as small as it
is; but they are also encouraged by the fact that the audience is
growing. Their efforts to satisfy a critical inmate population, to pacify
wary prison administrations, and still to reach and influence the outside public have resulted in an interesting and unusual communications venture.

Analysis and critical evaluation of the penal press's efforts to reach
its inside and outside audiences show meritorious results in each of the
basic areas of activity for communication media. It is generally agreed
that a communication medium, to fulfill its total obligation, should
inform, entertain, and *influence* its public. In each of these areas of
operation, both individually and taken as a group, prison publications
have shown some remarkable work.

THE PENAL PRESS AS AN INFORMATION MEDIUM

Editors of all penal publications, including the "literary" quarterlies, seem to feel an obligation to provide their readers with information. Virtually all prison publications contain some news, and
approximately nine out of ten of them devote more than half their
space to material of a general news nature, including sports.[6]

The quarterly magazines have an obvious time disadvantage in the
presentation of news and, in general, their results in this area are
rather inconsequential. Out-of-date sports results and standings are
often used, and pictures and coverage of entertainment events long
past use up valuable space in these magazines. The inmate population
probably has known of these activities and forgotten them by the time
such coverage appears, and most of the better magazines are concen-
trating their attention on creative efforts of inmates (see Chapter 5),
or depth studies of penology problems.[7] Some valuable interpreta-

6. Percentages presented in this chapter are from a content analysis of at
least four 1964 issues of 62 publications selected geographically (42 out of
the 50 states were represented) and from the larger institutions (all federal
and state prisons with a population of more than 2,000 were included).

7. Some administrators, such as Assistant Warden James Jordan of Maryland Penitentiary, supplement inmate magazines with weekly mimeographed
bulletins and special letters to provide faster dissemination of official news.
Institutional radio systems are also used effectively in many institutions.

tive articles on administrative policies are also being done. But for the magazines, and especially newspapers, that are published monthly or more frequently, the so-called spot news is an important element.

News items in a prison newspaper range from official announcements to murder stories. Considering the fact that the inmate publication's ability to transmit official information is one of the primary benefits to be derived by the administration, it is seemingly unusual that this type of material gets only a small amount of space. In no publication studied did official announcements take up more than 20 per cent of all space, and in 83 per cent of the publications they occupied less than 10 per cent of the space. In spite of its small space allotment, however, official news is a vital part of the prison publication; administration regulations and announcements by nature simply do not require too much space.

One of the more common methods for presenting official news is through a standing column written by the warden, as in the *San Quentin News,* or an associate warden, as in the Southern Michigan *Spectator.* The officials writing such columns use them to suit their own purposes; Warden Lawrence E. Wilson of San Quentin usually presents one general topic, often commending some aspect of inmate activity, while Deputy Warden Merwin S. Kircher's *Spectator* column usually contains details of regulations and warnings about infractions. Such columns are supplemented by separate news items for major policy changes. Commissary price lists, procedures for ordering newspapers and magazines, new educational and vocational opportunities, changes in dress regulations or recreation time, and mailing privileges are typical subjects for official announcements.

Most of the attention of a prison newspaper is devoted to inmate activities: sports events, movies and other entertainment, personal items, blood banks, school and organizational activities, hobbies, and the like. Sports events are thoroughly covered; movie schedules complete with typical ads and reviews are standard fare; inmate variety shows get profuse preliminary and follow coverage; personal recognition varies from "gossip column" notices to laudatory items for participation in blood drives and school activities; Alcoholics Anonymous, Synanon, Junior Chamber of Commerce, and the various religious organizations are subjects of many stories (or there may be a publication specifically produced by any one of these groups).

Internally, it would seem that the prison newspaper makes its greatest information contribution through the support it gives the special programs in the institution. Record blood collections, participation in cancer and other research projects, adoption of foreign children, and other similar worthwhile projects are thoroughly covered and boosted by the penal press. Recognition to the individual for participation in such events is valued in free society; to the convict in the nameless, number society of prison, such recognition is especially forceful. Without a publication in existence to support them, such civic activities would be much more difficult to encourage in the prison community.

A secondary information contribution results from the exchange of penal publications among institutions. Through the Penal Press, penal publications derive an obligation to mutually exchange issues and to grant reprint rights. Consequently, there is an unusual flow of information from one penal institution to another via the Penal Press. Inmates of a prison in Maryland know what is happening at a prison in California and vice versa. Thus the Penal Press forms an unusual information grapevine. And perhaps one of its strangest outgrowths is an expanded freedom for editors that has resulted from the practice of reprinting from other publications; many editors have found that subjects frowned upon by their censors if they originate locally, can be reprinted from other publications without complaint. Then, with the door to the subject open, it becomes legitimate material for the future.

This reprinting of one another's efforts has resulted in some self-criticism by prison editors who think abuse of the privilege has resulted in a few "canned" publications. Actually, the practice is well within reasonable limits; more than half the publications studied devoted at least 95 per cent of their space to local material. No publication used more than one-fourth of its space for reprints. Considering the side benefits received, reprinting within limitations is a worthy practice, especially if reprint material is carefully selected.

Although the prison press concentrates on the good things its readers do, there is occasional "bad" news too. Tight security keeps violence at a minimum in prison, and censorship would account for still further reductions in the prison press's coverage of such happenings. The fact that many prison publications severely criticize the outside press for its coverage of crime would also serve to explain the tendency to use only small amounts of such material. But stories of crime and violence have appeared and continue to appear in those penal press publications that have relative freedom and the desire to do a thorough job in covering their institutions. Even as early as 1916, *New Era* reported the killing of a guard in the main dining room by Robert L. Stroud, who later became known as "The Birdman of Alcatraz." Other such stories have appeared sporadically, including the following at the Nebraska Penal Complex in 1965: [8]

PENAL INMATE DIES
FROM KNIFE WOUND
Suspect Charged With First Degree Murder

Emzy Thompson, 37, from Beaumont, Texas, is dead. He died about 18 hours after he suffered a savage knife attack in his quarters last Sunday night.

Thompson was taken to the Pen-Unit hospital where it was determined that he needed immediate and expert medical attention, so he was transferred to Lincoln's St. Elizabeth Hospital, but the wound was a fatal one and he succumbed the following day.

Suspect Charged

Charles McClelland, 36, was charged Tuesday with Thompson's murder in Lancaster County District Court, because the suspect allegedly confessed to the attack moments afterwards.

The penalty for First Degree Murder upon conviction carries death by electrocution or life imprisonment.

McClelland is already under two life sentences that he received in 1948 for the double-slaying of the May family outside the entrance to Boys Town, Nebraska.

He was also charged with the knife-murder of print shop officer John Claussen in 1954, but was later acquitted.

Many prison publications would not be permitted to use such "unconstructive" material, but the Nebraska *Forum*, publisher of the

8. The *Forum*, December 4, 1965, p. 1.

above story, operates with considerably more freedom in such instances than most others. In 1964, when inmates staged a sitdown, the
usual printed edition of the *Forum* was replaced with a mimeographed
newsletter that noted the disturbance in this fashion:

> Publication of the April 25, 1964 edition of THE FORUM was
> sidelined as a direct result of the recent "no play, no work, no eat"
> sit-down strike conceived and perpetrated by a small percent of
> Nebraska's Penal Complex inmates during the three days of this
> week. Several of those involved were employed in the print shop
> and made impossible this week's issue.
>
> Although many inmates will be without a paper, it is the outside
> paid subscribers who were actually dealt a low blow.
>
> In an effort to assist those men belonging to various clubs,
> going to classification, or wanting to know what the movies are,
> THE FORUM has made available this little newsletter. . . ." [9]

Another newspaper with considerable freedom, the *Menard Time*,
won acclaim in 1965 for its handling of violence at the southern
Illinois prison. On Tuesday, November 23, a handful of convicts
turned on their guards in the prison dining room, killing three of them.
Outside newspapers and radio and television stations headlined the
incident as a riot; the *Menard Time* gave restrained but dramatic
attention to the tragedy by using all of its front page for this
editorial: [10]

AN EDITORIAL

Black Tuesday

> STUNNED, DUMBFOUNDED SILENCE gripped Menard. And only
> tragedy could have sparked it. It settled like a silk scarf over the
> prison, engulfing and absolute; for death is irrevocable. And
> death had taken three guards' lives in the line of duty.
>
> In ensuing hours, early unconfirmed reports prompted publica-
> tion of bold headlines in a minority of newspapers across the
> nation to banner the four-hour incident: "Convicts Riot; Slay
> Three Guards." And they were wrong.

9. "Strike Suspends Forum," *Forum Newsletter*, April 25, 1964, p. 1.
10. "Black Tuesday," *Menard Time*, December 1, 1965, p. 1.

LET'S SET THE RECORD STRAIGHT:

—A mere handful of prisoners participated.

—More than 1,000 prisoners—99.96 of those in the troubled area at the time—quietly filed from the shaken dining room and voluntarily returned to their cells one-half a block away in unsupervised lines without incident.

—Physical damage to the prison was one broken pane of glass, one split sack of beans and one dented saltshaker.

—Fifteen prisoners donated blood to wounded and dying officers—scores more offered blood, skin, organs and money for relatives of the deceased guards.

—Seventeen prisoners who were held hostages agreed among themselves to subdue the insurgents if they or three guard hostages were attacked.

—Three of the seventeen attempted to transfuse their blood into a wounded guard who they attended while being held hostages.

—Almost normal prison routine returned the next day.

—And sympathies of prisoners penetrated Menard's mass of concrete and steel, going to the wives and children of the slain guards.

THESE THINGS DON'T HAPPEN where there is a riot. They happen where there's a tragedy. The tragedy was in the death of three men; the tragedy was in the grief-stricken minds of widowed wives and fatherless children, the tragedy was in the incident.

The tragedy was Black Tuesday.

In carrying out its information function, the prison press is almost identical to the small-community press of the outside world. Organizations and activities are boosted with ample publicity, individual successes are recognized, and deaths are duly recorded. Emphasis is on the good things that occur, and institutional censorship levies some restrictions, but the bad is at least recognized as existing.

THE PRISON PRESS AS AN ENTERTAINMENT MEDIUM

Humor would seem to be out of place in prison, but the penal press never misses an opportunity to encourage a chuckle. On several occasions, editor Fred Tuggle of the Oklahoma Penitentiary *Eye Opener* has commented in his column that "My main ambition in life is to become an ex-convict." [11] Jim Kelly, editor of the Southern Michigan *Spectator*, began a column with, "This column was made possible by the untiring efforts of the Flint Police Department, the brilliant maneuvers of the Genosee County Prosecutor and the benevolence of a liberal magistrate." [12] Classified ads in the *Recount* of Colorado State Penitentiary included the following:

WANTED

Anyone driving to California and would like a travelling companion may contact me at this prison. Stop at the west wall, dim your lights, keep your motor running and be ready for a fast getaway . . . Richard Avery, CH 6

Young man to share (2) two bed bathroom. Half expenses, 9 to 10 year lease. Must have plenty of cigarettes. Contact Glimp, CH 6

SITUATION WANTED (Male Convict)

Alert man interested in learning financial end of business. Would like to work in place where lots of cash is handled. Would be willing to start at bottom and work up. Would be willing to start out just carrying money to bank . . . Lee Marlin, CH 7

TRADES

Would like to swap blows with prosecuting attorney . . . Dick Williams, CH 6 [13]

The ironic humor that permeates the prison press is perhaps its most striking characteristic to an outsider. In the effort to entertain their readers, prison editors have shown an amazing ability to see some humor in their dreary situation. They, the inmate population they represent, and their captors are all occasionally put on the receiving end of jokes. Cartoons, too, are standard entertainment fare, and many of them are of professional quality (see examples on pages 66, 97, and elsewhere). Some of the most popular and professional cartoons have been the work of Robert Matlock, whose prison odyssey brought his talent to a number of penal publications. [14] Matlock served as cartoonist for the *Agenda* of Washington State Prison prior to 1962, at which

11. Fred D. Tuggle, "133 Issues To Go," *Eye Opener* (November, 1963), p. 4.

12. Reprinted in *Menard Time*, March 1, 1966, p. 4.

13. "Classified Ads," *Recount* (Summer–Fall, 1963), p. 49.

14. "Bob Matlock Sends Latest Cartoons," the *Forum*, April 11, 1964, p. 3.

time he began drawing for the Nebraska *Forum*. He departed from the *Forum* staff in 1963, but provided that publication with another series of cartoons in 1964 while he was confined in the state reformatory at Pendleton, Indiana, and the state prison at Michigan City, Indiana. For Matlock and his counterparts, the favorite themes have been escape (the pole-vaulters and trampolinists at the wall were so common that the origin of these ideas is impossible to trace) and prison discipline. Men in chains, with only the tag line varying, were the subject of several cartoons.

Joke pages are still an integral part of several penal publications, but there appears to be a trend away from such canned humor. Many pre-World War II issues resembled joke books, but in the 1960's the pressure for space for more significant material was eliminating joke pages, and editors were looking for local humor to brighten their publications. Good little human interest stories with a light touch weren't overlooked, as this item from the Southern Michigan *Spectator* indicates:

Fly Watcher Club???
SMP Has Its Own

The regular meeting of "The Fly Watchers Club" was held last week. With cold weather coming on and fly watching season drawing to an end, the membership is rather upset and frustrated because it has been unable to solve its greatest problem.

After thousands of hours of concentrated watching, no one has been able to determine how a fly lands on the ceiling. So they're calling for "help." Can anyone tell us? When a fly is moving through the air, how does it get upside-down to land on the ceiling? Does it belly-roll sideways? Or does it go end up, front feet first?

After the regular business was taken care of, one of the maintenance motor men was awarded the "SMP Championship Fly Killers Trophy." He has accumulated the fantastic number of 109,906 dead flies, which he is proudly saving in a container to exhibit to non-believers.[15]

The *OPNews* turned criticism into a chuckle when it goofed by printing some erroneous track and field results that indicated that Ohio

15. The *Spectator*, October 6, 1964, p. 4.

Penitentiary runners had shattered world records. An irate reader complained: "The OPNews is a publication that reflects part of prison life. Surely it was a mistake to publish times that were fantastic. The times published would make the best runners in the country look foolish. Being a former track man myself, I feel that this hurts the sport." To this attack, the *OPNews* responded:

> After hearing repercussions from near and far about the extremely fast time turned in by a few of our fleet-footed track stars in the Fourth of July Track Meet, the OPNews is ready to admit that we goofed.
>
> While the OPNews is responsible for the validity of everything printed herein, we have to admit that we never checked the time on these events, nor did we check the length of the track. We also admit that we are not familiar with the various track records and, consequently, had no idea that some national track records had been broken (according to our track and timer).
>
> While we offer our apologies to our many faithful readers for this unforgivable error, we did learn that the two men responsible for taking the unofficial time and laying out the unofficial track have previously been convicted of felonies; one is an ex-armed robber and the other is an ex-con artist.[16]

Longer feature articles, some based on fact and others primarily concocted by the writer's imagination, also add a light touch. The Colorado *Recount* published an elaborate convict's calendar, including lists of famous people born each month and famous events of the month.[17] Famous people born included Jack the Ripper, Bluebeard, Albert Anastasia, Baby Face Nelson, Ma Barker, Benedict Arnold, Machine Gun Kelly, Lucrezia Borgia, Judas Iscariot, and Jesse James. Famous events recorded month-by-month included the Brink's Robbery, St. Valentine's Day Massacre, Crucifixion of Christ, invention of the guillotine, invention of the electric chair, and the burning of Rome.

Recognition, in similar vein, was given to the "shop of the month" from within the prison (i.e., Fingerprint shop: "Where tints of your prints are sent to pertinent governments for comment on the extent of

16. "Did We Goof?" *OPNews*, July 31, 1965, p. 2.
17. *Recount* (Christmas, 1963), pp. 16–17, 19–20.

frequent imprisonment you underwent and in the event they meant to prevent your descent from punishment to implement a document of their intent. Now you may resent their argument that it's not meant for your detriment but don't vent your dissent in an insolent and belligerent lament or you'll get sent to the cement tenement to repent.")

Ironic humor is not the only element of features, however. Interesting articles on music and other arts, on unusual hobbies of prisoners, on historical subjects, travel, and virtually every conceivable subject find their way to penal press pages.

An editor's column, plus perhaps one or two others, is also a basic part of the entertainment offering of most penal papers. Some columns tended to be on sentimental subjects, some on specialized interests, such as music, but some were also humorous. Jim Kelly, as editor of the Marquette [Michigan] *Weekly Progress* before his transfer to Southern Michigan Prison, entertained his readers with a column resembling the patter of a night club comedian:

THE BOSS
by
Jim Kelly

I met her in a revolving door and I've been going around with her ever since. I call her Jackson because she looks like a stone wall. And she calls me Pilgrim because everytime I went out with her I made a little progress. I remember how we used to walk down the street and all the boys would whistle at her. Half the time I didn't know whether I was out with a girl or a dog. Ah, but I loved the ground her stockings dragged over. She had a very unique figure. If she hadn't had housemaid's knee her legs wouldn't have had any shape at all. Oh, but it's true. We had our quarrels but we always decided to kiss and make up. She got the kiss and I got the make-up. It was love at first sight so I married her. Then I wished I had taken a second look. Without knowing it I had taken my first step towards divorce—marriage. As we walked down the aisle she had a bouquet of roses on her arm and I had Four Roses on my breath. . . .[18]

Most editors, however, used their columns for what they considered to be the most important function of the penal press: to *influence* their

18. *Weekly Progress*, May 22, 1964, p. 4.

readers. In the final analysis, the entire content of penal publications is
directed toward this end.

THE PENAL PRESS AS A MEDIUM OF INFLUENCE

Penal publications are similar in many respects to the "house organs" of corporations and other organizations of the outside world.
Just as house organs are, the prison publications are produced by an
organization with the intent of promoting that organization's well-
being. Consequently, their opinion-molding function is dominant in
their operation—or it should be. There is no denying the fact that
there is an axe to be ground, and that the axe is two-edged. Penal
publications can be an effective medium of influence among the inmate
population, and they can bring the problems of prisons and prisoners
to the general public in order to create a better understanding and to
bring about improvements in our prison system.

The opinion-molding function should be paramount for penal publications because the investment of funds and other resources in their
operation is solely motivated by the desires of inmates and administrators to change the attitudes of others. Penal publications try to inform
and to entertain *in order to influence*.

Influencing the Inmate Audience

Internal house organs in a free society exist to create harmonious
relations between management and employees. Their content is geared
to convincing employees that the company for which they work is a
good company—that it is in the employees' best interest to stay with
the company and put forth maximum effort in their jobs. There is
enough similarity in the basic character of prison publications that
they are often called "prison house organs," but the differences between prison society and corporate organizations cannot be overlooked. These differences make the potential of prison publications
even greater than that of the free-world house organs.

Prisons exist for three purposes: to punish wrongdoers for their crimes and thus, hopefully, deter others from doing wrong; to protect society by segregating dangerous individuals under sufficient security to prevent repetition of crimes by them; and to rehabilitate the wrongdoer and return him to society as a law-abiding and responsible citizen. It is not our purpose here to debate the relative merits of each of these; instead it is to try to determine the place of the press within a society structured with these goals in mind. Theoretically at least, the worth of the prison press can be measured in terms of how effective it is in helping prisons achieve their goals.

For its aid in accomplishing the first of these purposes—the punishment of wrongdoers—the penal press must be given a failing grade. Penal publications are not helpful as tools of punishment. They may be of some slight assistance in the end goal of punishment—to deter crime—but not sufficiently to justify their existence. Autobiographical articles are occasionally written and presented by inmates to warn others of the folly of crime, and if they reached the right readers they could conceivably help sway these readers away from the commission of crimes. On the whole, however, penal publications cannot be justified on the basis of punishment or crime deterrence related to it.

With regard to the second of the three purposes—that of protecting society—the penal press deserves a somewhat better grade. Although it is true that criminals could be securely segregated by locking them in individual enclosures and providing them with the essentials of life through barred doors, this efficient system has been considered too inhumane as routine treatment. Consequently, even in maximum security installations, prisoners are given some freedom to move about, and to engage in work and recreation. With even the limited freedoms that are granted, however, come problems of morale and security. Discontent and unrest have, unfortunately, reached the boiling point in several institutions, resulting in destruction of life and property. Any available means for keeping morale at the necessary level for orderly maintenance of prison life would, therefore, seem to be of value.

Herein arise the differences between penal publication readers and house organ readers. Inmates are not in prison by their own choosing and they have no career motivation to inspire them to constructive effort within the organization; they are, as a group, antisocial. Any individuals would be difficult to hold in confinement; those who have committed crimes are especially hard to channel into orderly behavior. Their antagonism toward *any* authority is even stronger against an authority that controls their confinement. Existing in this kind of a situation, the penal press faces more difficulties than an outside house organ but, if successful, can be of even greater value.

Prison administrators and convict editors alike agree that the penal press can succeed in building and maintaining inmate morale. As a basic objective of the penal press, morale ranked second only to providing an outlet for creativity, according to prison administrators surveyed; approximately 63 per cent considered this to be one of their primary goals. Several administrators and inmates have also acclaimed the penal press as a "safety valve" through which bitterness can be permitted to escape without explosion. Its value as a means for learning of inmate dissatisfaction has also been noted.

How can the penal press most effectively perform its morale-building role? Here the prison publication is mainly a catalyst, not the primary substance. Specific programs are provided to occupy the mental and physical energies of inmates, and it is the job of the inmate periodical to promote these programs so that they will succeed. The use of libraries can be and is encouraged by the penal publication through book reviews, library columns, and similar material. Educational opportunities are thoroughly covered and promoted. The success of recreational programs is stimulated by the recognition that comes from stories lauding individual performances, and from publication of individual and team standings. Stories of the success of inmate artists and craftsmen encourage other spare-time activity of that nature. Coverage of the various shops and industries within the prison gives helpful recognition, too.

It should be rather obvious here that the work of the penal press in encouraging worthwhile activities to build morale leads naturally to its most important internal activity: that of an aid to rehabilitation.

Wherever strong emphasis on the goal of rehabilitation in prisons exists, the penal publication should be strong and successful. In a basically negative society, the penal press is one of the few positive elements. Assuming that there is a need to change the behavior standards and thinking patterns of prison inmates, what forces are there in a prison society to bring this about? From his peers, the prisoner can be expected mainly to have his negative attitudes reinforced, rather than changed. Vocational training helps prepare him for gainful employment, an important factor in preparing him for return to society *if his attitude directs him toward worthwhile employment.* From books and educational opportunities he can get proper direction, *if he is motivated to read and enroll in classes.* A positive attitude and properly channeled motivation are essential to rehabilitation, and it would seem that there is an unusual opportunity for a periodical, *accepted by the inmate as his,* and *dealing with his problems in a constructive fashion,* to have a favorable influence upon him. The italics here indicate the two essentials for success of the penal publication in the rehabilitative process—high credibility with inmates and a constructive approach. These ingredients often conflict, and they point to the dilemma that presents the greatest challenge to prison administration. To afford an inmate publication with sufficient freedom that it wins the acceptance of the population—while guaranteeing that the publication will be constructive in approach—requires special effort, but it is being done. (See Chapter 6 for a pertinent discussion.)

Literally hundreds of news stories, columns, feature articles, and even cartoons could be reprinted here from the penal press to illustrate its work as a constructive medium of influence within prison walls. The better prison publications are full of good examples, but three items—two editorials and an excerpt from a column—should suffice to make the point.

The first editorial is from the Minnesota *Prison Mirror* of August 13, 1965. It appeared on a page that included the following: two inmate letters of thanks, one in appreciation of treatment received at the prison hospital and the other addressed to fellow inmates who had contributed blood for the writer, a leukemia victim; a short news item on the Minnesota Justice Department's stand against capital punishment; continuation from page one of a story about a court decision affecting suspects' rights; biographies of three children "adopted" by residents of the penitentiary; and a column. An excerpt from the column follows the editorial:

Editorial

It looks like August is donation month at Minnesota State Prison. Unless you're a complete deadbeat, read on . . .

BLOOD: As you know the Red Cross Bloodmobile will be here Aug. 31. Men who wish to donate should send a kite to Bruce McManus, classification supervisor.

Nine of the 16 men on the print shop roster have already signed to give blood. Two of the seven who didn't won't be here Aug. 31.

One non-donor is over 60, sickly, dried up and shell-shocked. Another is a weight lifter. Two others are bitter. And one is a sissy.

Although we don't expect the other shops to do as well as the print shop, we'd like to know if any other shop has signed over 50 per cent.

SAVE THE CHILDREN: Elsewhere in the *Mirror* is a story on three children we've "adopted."

It costs $420 a year to support the three of them.

Somebody will come around to your cell tomorrow night (Saturday, Aug. 14) and ask if you want to donate. If you live in cellhall "B," that "somebody" will be John Azzone. Roy Gadbois will see you in the cellhall "A," Harley Sorenson in "D," Fred Helm at the Farm, and Dick Harding at the Men's Dormitory.

If you like kids, give a buck or two—or two bits if you're caught short. If you don't like kids, don't give anything.

SMOKES FOR ST. PETER: As most of you know, there used to be a barrel put out on canteen nights for cigarettes to be sent to the men at the security hospital at St. Peter.

The barrel plan didn't work out too well. Not many men put cigarettes in it.

Some of you have been in the security hospital and know what it's like down there. It's no picnic. What makes it worse is that the inmates don't get paid anything—and that means no cigarettes unless they have someone on the outside to send them money.

Or unless we help them.

We can and should help them. Therefore, whoever comes to your cell tomorrow night for a Save the Children donation will also ask you to give a few pennies for the men at Minnesota Security Hospital.

Don't give much. Two bits or a half dollar is plenty—if everybody gives. And everybody should give. There's not much excuse for not helping your fellow inmates.

The money will be sent to Mrs. Dona Macias, head nurse, and Ward Marsh, recreation director, at the security hospital. Both of these people are solid and they're for the cons (ask the guys who know them). They'll spend the money wisely.

They'll give us a full accounting of how the money is spent, and we'll print it in the *Mirror*.[19]

In approach and language, the editorial represents an insider speaking to his peers, not an outsider preaching to some inferiors. On the same page, columnist Rex Fletcher included as one of his eight items the following personal commentary:

We are always a little sad to read about young kids getting into trouble, because we know what's in store for most of them: a lifetime of suffering, misery, deadly monotony, and finally, friendless oblivion.

When we see a young fellow come into a prison, we travel backward in time and see ourselves as we must have been 30 years ago—tough, arrogant, bull-headed, and a real know-it-all. We know exactly what most of them will be like 30 years from now, after they have served most of those years in prison. They will be quiet, subdued, reflective, serious, polite, and very, very regretful—perhaps even remorseful—as they look back on a completely wasted life.

A few years ago, a prison psychologist asked us what we had accomplished during our long years in prison. We thought for awhile, then replied: "Well, sir, we've kept from going insane."

Compare the potential effectiveness of these examples to the lectures and admonitions of well-meaning but forever remote "outsiders"! The entire page constituted one good, strong, constructive push in the right direction for its readers. And for newspapers like the *Mirror*, this performance is typical.

Another forceful publication is the *San Quentin News*, source of the final editorial example. The *News* takes no "namby-pamby," "goody-goody" approach in its columns; it has had a tradition of straight-talking, hard-hitting editors. The following editorial was submitted as a letter to the *News*. The introductory note is by *News* editor Cary Johanneson, a fine writer who must have winced at the letter-writer's

19. *Prison Mirror*, August 13, 1965, p. 2.

grammar and jargon, while realizing that this roughness would be a major determinant of the letter's effectiveness.

A TASTE OF PHILOSOPHY . . .

(Editor's note: The following letter was received by the *San Quentin News* from an inmate who shall remain unidentified. It's genuine and you might say the writer is "telling it like it is.")

This is wrote for the young convict between the ages of 18 and 25. For the convict who is sent to San Quentin with the idea that in order to be considered a "regular" or "good people" by other convicts he must display a hostile attitude toward the "bulls" or he feels he must swagger around the yard with a chip on his shoulder and a shank in his pocket.

As we all know, a "regular" is a convict who isn't a "rat" or a "punk" and who is respected by other "regulars." But just how many "regulars" are there? Very darn few, Buddy, believe me.

The regulars aren't understood by the officials because there are too few of us to worry about, therefore we have a hard row to hoe. They can't rap to us because we won't let them. We think that by seeking their help in whatever program they have to offer is "sniveling." So what? Well here's so what . . . we end up in prison for five or six years when we should have been out of this dump in 18 or 24 months.

So if our "code" won't let us go to the "bulls" and try to get out then let's go to each other. Find some old timer who is a regular and have him run it down to you. He may tell you to go to school or learn a trade. Well, go to school and learn a trade. That don't make you a rat. He may tell you if some "bull" "bugs" you just keep your big mouth shut. Well shut it, that don't make you a "punk." The funny part about it, "before you or I go home," we are going to have to do these things anyway. So why prolong it?

Would you rather be standing on the big yard in your "bona-roos" fat mouthing some "bull" or would you like to be laying on some beach soft-talking some blonde? I know a lot of "regulars" who are out on the streets doing just that. This joint is nothing.

Just stop and look at yourself. Are you a big wheeler and dealer on the big yard? Do you run around in a gang? Do you have a "shank"? If you do then you're a fool and it don't take no guts to be a fool. Folsom is full of regulars doing life because they were fools like you when they were young.

I know because I'm one of those fools. The biggest fool of them all. I came here when I was 18 years old. I had a 6 to 14. I thought to be a "regular" you had to pack a shank, own a cell full of cigarettes and hate everybody who represented authority. I didn't know then that you could learn a trade or go to school and act like a man and still be a regular. I know now that I'm 9 years too late. I'm 27 years old. I parlayed my 14 top to life. I got nine solid years in. I got four and a half years in the Adjustment Center and isolation and at the time of this writing I'm doing 29 days in isolation and I'm going to outside court on a beef which calls for the gas chamber. Big deal! I'm a regular all right, a regular fool. Don't you be one.[20]

In spite of agreement with the effectiveness of these examples, one might ask why not just duplicate such material occasionally and post it on a bulletin board, or read it over the public address system, or have custodial officers relay it? Why bother with a newspaper or magazine? The answer is, of course, that a periodical, by virtue of the fact that it is published at regular intervals, has some definite advantages. Believability is necessary for persuasion, and repetition can aid believability. An inmate publication, with sufficient freedom to gain acceptance by its audience, and the advantage of periodic exposure in the commonly accepted newspaper or magazine form, has unusual potential in the prison setting.

The Role of Special Publications

Even in the earliest prison publications, old "John Barleycorn" was cited as one of the chief contributors to the downfall of those in prison. And since that time, a constant barrage condemning excessive drinking of alcohol has been maintained in the penal press. There is no doubt that large numbers of convicts are what they are because they drank too much, then engaged in an act of violence or got too eager in writing checks. Today drug addiction, directly and indirectly, takes hundreds into prison yearly. Whether addicts are confined because they were caught violating a narcotics law or because they committed

20. *San Quentin News*, February 3, 1966, p. 2.

crimes to get a supply of drugs, prime responsibility for their actions lies in the drug habit. In the modern prison with serious effort directed toward rehabilitation, organized programs to combat these causes of crime are commonplace. Alcoholics Anonymous, Synanon, and Checks Anonymous groups are so active in many prisons that they publish regular periodicals of their own. These self-help groups, plus some religious and civic organizations, such as the Holy Name Society and the Junior Chamber of Commerce, publish a total of 113 periodicals in correctional institutions.

These specialized inmate publications are not glamorous or exciting to an outsider, but they are a commendable facet of the rehabilitation work of the penal press. They strike at the basic sources of difficulty for many prisoners, and consequently can be of special assistance. In some instances they are the only inmate publications in an institution, but usually they exist in addition to general inmate periodicals. Their content is what one would expect; they vigorously follow the precepts of their organizations and try, through repetition of personal accounts, to show the individual's responsibility to overcome his problem and to provide the inspiration that comes from knowing it can be done.

The Penal Press as an External Influence

America's first prison newspaper was established as a medium to influence the outside public. Today's strong desire of convict editors to make their publications a more potent outside influence thus brings the penal press to the completion of a cycle. After years of concentration on their obligations to the inmate audience, prison editors now believe, as Al Nussbaum put it, that "the primary audience is *outside* the walls."

There is no doubt that the penal press can be of great service in this area—service to prison inmates, prison administrations, and society in general. The public is inclined to neglect penal institutions. Other syphons of the public monies usually are more appealing, and the prison system seems forever doomed to inadequate facilities and operating revenues. Lack of public attention to prison conditions and to the warnings and requests of prison administrators often means that pennies saved ultimately result in dollars lost through higher recidivism rates and destruction from violence. Public understanding of modern penological thought, and of the means needed to put new ideas into practice, would benefit everyone.

Some institutions still restrain their inmate publications from general outside circulation; only persons having some direct connection with these institutions are permitted on the mailing list. This practice is giving way, however, to some definite efforts to increase the range of the outside audience. Where the effort has been made, reasonable success has resulted. In 1966, the Southern Michigan *Spectator* reported that, in the previous five months, outside subscriptions had doubled over the previous year. The *Menard Time* raised its outside circulation to more than 5,500; the *Mentor* reaches 5,350 outsiders; *New Era*, 3,000; the Iowa *Presidio*, 2,341; Indiana State Prison's *Lake Shore Outlook* and *Encourager*, 2,150 and 2,250 respectively; and the *Atlantian*, 2,000. Several others reach more than 1,000 outsiders, but the total external circulation of about 72,000 is distressingly small.

There are some encouraging factors about this external circulation, however. It is growing; there undoubtedly is a substantial "pass along" readership; and the recipients include many persons of influence. Judges, public officials, educators, clergymen, doctors, students, lawyers, writers, and other opinion leaders are prominent among the penal press readers. These letters to the editor in one issue of *Stretch* of Kansas State Prison give some indication of this readership:

DEAR EDITOR:

. . . I am a Kansan in school in Pennsylvania; other students read STRETCH here when I get it. It speaks well for our state.

TIM MILLER
CROZIER THEOLOGICAL SEMINARY
CHESTER, PENN.

DEAR EDITOR:

I find your magazine tremendously interesting and pass it on to my friends. It sure helps in a better understanding of our mutual problems.

REP. DONALD A. BELL
1475 LIEUNIT STREET
WICHITA, KANSAS

DEAR EDITOR:

I am very pleased to receive the magazine, as it gives another side of institutional life that I think people should know about. I have used material from other issues and am enclosing the latest, used from the December issue. It's a good magazine.

PATRICIA ANDERSON
Women's Editor
INDIO DAILY NEWS
PALM DESERT, CAL.

DEAR EDITOR:

I am now serving as a chaplain in the U. S. Navy. While I am no longer living in Kansas, I am very interested in the program at K.S.P. Please keep the STRETCH coming to me.

EDWARD L. HUGHES
3109 CONQUISTA AVENUE
LONG BEACH, CAL.

DEAR EDITOR:

I find the magazine most useful in communicating to my students some feeling for the realities of confinement and the problems faced by both prisoners and staff. Since this is most important in education of future framers of public opinion in correctional matters, I regard this as a most worthy service.

DR. ELMER H. JOHNSON
CENTER FOR STUDY OF CRIME,
DELINQUENCY AND CORRECTION,
SOUTHERN ILLINOIS UNIVERSITY,
CARBONDALE, ILL.

DEAR EDITOR:

. . . I obtained the Dec. issue, and I did enjoy reading it. I feel it has helped me to understand somewhat better a few of the problems that the inmates have. I would like to continue receiving it.

I believe we on the outside need a better understanding in order to be of help to those who are released, to adjust back to a normal, useful life. I speak as a mother and a wife, and do sincerely want to help . . .

MARGIE GENT
1421 GENT
MANHATTAN, KANS.

DEAR EDITOR:

You are to be congratulated on a fine, forthright presentation. I would be interested in your suggestions to the Legislature as to how to best approach the prison problem. What should the relationship be between rehabilitation and punishment?

> SENATOR KEITH G. SEBILIUS
> CARTER BUILDING
> NORTON, KANS.

DEAR EDITOR:

It is gratifying to know that the Editor and his staff are . . . performing a distinguished service not only for themselves and companions, but to us "outsiders."

The talent, creative ability and articulate interest all of you have in penal affairs, rehabilitation, humor, sports, law, et cetera, speaks well for all of you.

Your publication is made available to my clients in the reception room of my office and, frankly, it creates a great deal of favorable comment . . .

> J. P. GENUSA [21]

Please remember that these letters are all from one issue; they were not selected from various issues to create the varied audience they represent. And this page is not an exception; one "Dear Editor" page of *New Era* contained letters from a U. S. Senator, the Governor of Alaska, two college English instructors, three clergymen, two directors of art galleries, a university poet-in-residence, three magazine editors, the director of an Israeli university, a curator of rare books, an advertising agency representative, and several other readers.[22]

To these outside readers, and hopefully to more and more "ordinary voters," the penal press is attempting to present a multifaceted message. First of all, it is trying to get across the idea that prisoners *are people*, not some special breed of animal that, once caged, should be completely forgotten. Secondly, it is trying to gain acceptance of the principle that penal institutions should be dedicated to rehabilitation rather than punishment. In this connection, it is attempting to change

21. "Letters to the Editor," *Stretch* (February, 1966), pp. 7–8.
22. "Dear Editor," *New Era* (Summer, 1964), p. 105.

public attitudes toward parolees and discharged prisoners—to eliminate the "ex-con" stigma as a handicap to readjustment.

The editors who are concerned with reaching the outside public use
every weapon in their arsenal to get their message across. In trying to
show that "we are people, too," these editors rely on news about the
worthy activities and projects of inmates, but they also make a direct
"pitch" in columns and editorials. Scores of articles, though the words
are different, are on this same theme. Typical of these is the following
from the Marquette [Michigan] *Weekly Progress:*

> . . . Contrary to the opinion of many, convicts ARE people.
>
> There are short ones, tall ones, medium size ones, young ones,
> old ones, and at least one who is considered by all to be 42 and
> lovely. There are intelligent ones, dumb ones, mediocre ones and
> exceptional ones. There are happy ones and there are also sad
> ones. They are just people.
>
> Why is it that one person steals and the other doesn't? Why is it
> that some follow the so-called straight and narrow and the other
> doesn't? What is the big difference between the crooked and the
> honest? Is it in the way they think? If this is so, then why does
> one think one thing and the other something altogether different?
>
> Come to think of it, why does anyone think the way that they
> do? Why are one person's feelings bent in one direction and the
> other's in another?
>
> Do convicts think: Do they have feelings? Do they love? Hate?
> Like? Wonder? Rage? Do they think and feel what they think
> about? What causes one person to be positive and the other
> negative? One to hate and one to love? One to feel superior and
> the other inferior? One to have confidence and the other not?
> Where are thinking habits formed? Are we born with them or are
> they developed? Does society have anything to do with the way an
> individual thinks? Feels? Acts? Does anyone take himself into a
> corner and say, "I am going to be an honest man," or "I am going
> to be a thief"?
>
> There comes a night in every con's life when he is read out . . .
> when he is ear-phoned out . . . when he is hobby-crafted out . . .
> when he has to think and travel down his own personal memory
> lane. This happens more often than you would realize but not as
> frequently as some would hope.

What happens to a con on a night like this? Does he take a stroll in the park? Attend a movie? Play with the kids? Or does he wait for the guard to make his final count and the lights to go out? Does he finally bed himself down in his little "beddy-bye," with his smoking handy and brace himself for a long go of it?

Does he think of the months to go? The years? Maybe the eternity? Does he think of old loves that have been won, and lost? Does he think of the marriage that went down the drain? The children that have been forever removed?

Does he finally reach deep down within and with a burning resentful rage, utter the almost defiant, curse-like prayer that must blast the very gates of heaven? Why? Why? Why?

Convicts ARE TOO people.[23]

Perhaps the most important development in the operation of the penal press in the last three decades is associated with the other facet of its external effort: to further the concept of rehabilitation rather than punishment as the goal of penal institutions. With some of the better publications as leaders, the penal press has embarked on a serious effort to analyze criminal behavior, the effects of confinement, and the potential for rehabilitation. Studies in greater depth than ever before attempted are now becoming fairly common. Results of these studies are offered, not as a panacea for all the ills of crime and punishment, but as the only *truly authentic* views of the problem because they come from its very source.

In the words of *Raiford Record* editor, Clyde Brown:

Ours is not a story that can be gotten adequately from textbooks on criminology by so-called experts, who at best have delved into the subject as theorizing outsiders, even though in some instances they were practicing psychologists, [they were] outsiders nevertheless. No man in an outside position can properly understand and define the inside! Anticipating the objection that we are not qualified, we reply that the doctor always asks the patient: "What is the matter? . . . Where does it hurt?"—not requiring or even

23. Tom Redgate, "Suffer, Suffer Little Cons," *Weekly Progress*, November 22, 1963, p. 3.

wishing him to be a doctor in order to supply the needed answers.[24]

Editor Brown's words were part of the introduction to a twelve-page symposium, "Our Closed World," that included the views of two recidivists attempting to explain the causes of their criminal behavior and the effect on them of their prior sentences. In the first issue of the *Interpreter*, the magazine that replaced *Recount* at Colorado State Penitentiary in 1966, a series called "The Murder Syndrome" was started. Each episode, the magazine said, would have "another thinking man 'doing life' for murder take you behind the shutters of his mind to contribute what he can to help de-fuse the walking time bombs roaming our streets and highways this and every night." [25]

These examples are perhaps more spectacular and attention-getting than most penal press articles, but there have been many others just as interesting and significant. Articles have been based on questionnaires (*Presidio* editor Robert Bauman got data from thirty-three states to publish a series on employment opportunities for men with criminal records) and interviews (*New Era* has used an article on the causes of delinquency that was based on the questioning of 700 inmates with juvenile records), as well as the dramatic personal accounts. The subjects tackled by the penal press as it attempts to enlarge its new dimension of depth writing are far ranging. Some of the favorite subjects for crusades have already been achieved, others have not. They include: half-way houses, pre-release programs, prisoner furloughs, abolishment of capital punishment, more lenient parole standards, conjugal visits, uncensored mail (and penal publications), abolishment of solitary confinement, and the right to serve in military forces wherever they are in action.

The underlying point in most of the crusades is the same: prisons as they now exist can only be expected to turn out men who will return, again and again, to confinement. Changes must be made if prisons are ever to be expected to rehabilitate their inmates. An editorial by Al Rutledge, published in the Maryland *Courier* just a few months before inmates there rioted and did $200,000 damage to the ancient and

24. "Our Closed World," *Raiford Record* (January–February, 1961), p. 3.
25. "The Murder Syndrome," the *Interpreter* (May, 1966), p. 42.

crowded prison, is one of the strongest expressions of this point of view:

> In his "Ballad of Reading Gaol" Oscar Wilde wrote ". . . the vilest deeds/ Like poison weeds/ Bloom well in prison air/ It is only what is good in men/ That wastes and withers there." In these twenty-four words he gave to penology, criminology, sociology and a host of other "ologies" what half a century of intense investigation has failed to do or, at best, has only just begun to discover—that good adjustment in the prison atmosphere, is in effect, submission to the influence of "the vilest deeds" and that, by its very nature, prison is the sire of recidivism.
>
> In two sentences Wilde said what the social sciences teach in volumes: "Man is a product of his environment, his behavior the expression of his experience."
>
> The paradox of the prison system is: The inmate is expected to adjust to the codes of the society from which he came. However, prison is an environment that works its influence in concentrated specifics. Altruisms and abstractions aside, the inmate comes directly under the influence of "prison air."
>
> He must serve a part of his life in the soil that breeds the poison weed. Society says that for this period he must be punished. And, indeed, he will be. But for ten, fifteen or twenty years? Not hardly! Survival of the fittest will continue to drive the man, despite the shackles or chains. Prison intensifies the will to survive. He must either go mad, vegetate or adapt himself, by choice or chance, to the conditions under which he lives. The punishment must be lessened. In either case prison becomes the home and the society to which he belongs.
>
> Prison rules are substantial guidelines for civil obedience and the prisoner who satisfactorily adjusts to them will be better equipped to get out of prison, stay out of prison and be a better citizen. Theoretically this is true, but rules and regulations are not the only elements permeating "prison air" and they're certainly not the most influential. To the prisoner who views them only as instruments made to keep him in the lowly condition of prisoner they have no influence at all.
>
> The basic issue is the prisoner's physical, spiritual, and mental needs. He's frightened and there's no place to run; he's angry and can only strike at himself; he's contrite but few people care; he's

arrogant but must bow to other men; he lusts for love and has no woman! Prison, its rules and regulations deny him all the means to satisfy those needs. What's more, they're propagated by the system, of which he is not a part. But we find in prison codes of defiance, home-made booze (jumpsteady), and homosexuality. Here, then, are the "poison seeds" and he is a part of the soil in which they grow.

If he's prison-adjusted he's prison-oriented. Put him in the outside world and, chances are, you have a recidivist: a man responding to situations in a manner proven successful to him, behaving according to his experience. Hate and defiance cannot be expressed in terms of human decency and love.

He gets sleepy at the same hour each night, he sleeps confined to a three foot expanse on a double bed, he's clumsy with silver and chinaware; authorities say, "Don't worry, he just has to adjust." The body has been orientated. Orientation of the mind is not considered.

The fact is, society asks that the offender repent and adjust to the conditions of the normal society during his prison stay. On the other hand, the prison system requires that the convict obey and adjust to conditions alien to normal society. Of course, this man is expected to be a better citizen. But what, in "prison air" remotely resembles the principles of a good homelife: community obligations, the responsibilities of a husband, a father, a neighbor, a man? Nothing!

Prison's ultimate service is isolation of those convicted of felonies. It is the limbo of human society where those convicted are confined. To conjure up virtues of glorious rejuvenation as its end is folly.

Look then, to the recidivist as a "product of his environment" and if he "behaves in a manner expressive of his experiences," he has adjusted and the system's end is accomplished.[26]

Rutledge's editorial is in many ways a summary of the message that the penal press is trying to get to the outside public. The specific changes that are advocated are merely parts of the basic change that is sought: the shift in emphasis from punishment to rehabilitation. Herman K. Spector, in his *Bibliography on Criminology-Penology and*

26. "Editorial," the *Courier* (February, 1966), p. 1.

Related Subjects, expressed the goals of the prison press well when he said, in part, that it sought: (1) "The admission, after proof, that men *can* be permanently rehabilitated to useful community life"; and (2) "the adoption of socializing and rehabilitative measures behind prison walls—followed by equally progressive after care."

"Toward these ends," Spector said, "the prison press is as solemnly dedicated as a labor press is dedicated to the cause of labor, and the combined American free press is dedicated to the preservation of that freedom to which it owes its life." [27]

27. Herman K. Spector, *Bibliography on Criminology-Penology and Related Subjects* (New York City Department of Corrections: 1944), p. 179.

Anonymous, The *Courier* (Maryland State Penitentiary; Summer, 1964), p. 41

CHAPTER 5

Prison Publications as an Outlet for Creative Self-Expression

I can stand any kind of hardships or privations on the outside, but I am utterly unable to continue the life I lead here. I know all the arguments that could be advanced as to why I should endure it, but I have reached the limit of endurance. It will be better for everyone else and a thousand times better for me to end the trouble instead of dragging it out longer . . .—C. Alphonso Smith, O. HENRY BIOGRAPHY, 1916.

ABOVE ARE THE WORDS of Convict 30644 just three weeks after the heavy gates of the Ohio Penitentiary had slammed shut behind him. The indignities of prison life pressed down on his spirit with overpowering force. The shaved head, the physical inspections, the loss of personal identity, and a host of other degradations combined with a depressing sense of shame to make his five-year sentence for embezzlement seem beyond the reach of his endurance.

But Convict 30644 was bank teller William Sidney Porter of Austin, Texas, who had been confined to prison on April 25, 1898, and emerged three years and three months later as O. Henry, master short-story writer. Something during his confinement had brought him from the depth of suicidal despondency to a place of prominence in American literature.

More than any other individual, O. Henry has stirred a ripple of curiosity about the ability of prisons to serve as breeding grounds for creative genius. Other great men of the arts and politics have provided additional impetus to such speculation. Nowhere is more attention given to the prison backgrounds of great men of history than in the penal press. References are so frequent to Socrates, St. Paul, Christopher Columbus, Galileo Galilei, Thomas More, John Bunyan, Daniel Defoe, Fyodor Dostoevsky, Oscar Wilde—and O. Henry—that imprisonment seems to be a requisite for greatness.

The length of the list of the great prisoners is enough, in itself, to place a faint stamp of credibility on the idea and to attract some outside attention to it.[1] Any study of such a list, however, immediately reveals that for most of these men it was not prison that brought them greatness; it was greatness that brought them to prison. Their confinement came because their ideas were contrary to the established order, because they could articulate their ideas and consequently were a danger to authority. In short, their crimes were political and not antisocial in nature.

From the long list of early prison writers, Oscar Wilde and O. Henry would be most closely akin to the staff writers of American prison magazines who seek to bask in the reflected glory of those two men. Wilde's crime was nonpolitical; he was sentenced to two years for homosexuality. O. Henry's confinement for embezzlement certainly had no political overtones. Wilde, however, had achieved extraordinary success as a writer before his conviction. Prison undoubtedly had a strong influence on him, but it tended to break him rather than to make him as a writer. Although he produced *De Profundis* in prison and under great handicaps, it alone probably would not have brought him lasting fame. Out of history, only O. Henry remains as a legitimate

1. In his anthology of literature written in prison, *The Great Prisoners,* Isidore Abramowitz has presented a fascinating collection starting with the *Apology* of Socrates and ending with the World War II period. His list of prison authors is like a roll call of the great men of history.

source of consolation and inspiration for prison writers; his leap from obscurity to national attention was achieved while he was in confinement.

Other convict writers of more recent years have tended to keep alive the concept that prison nurtures creative talent. Until the 1920's, prison writers were pretty much "becalmed in the doldrums of official inertia and public neglect." [2] Then H. L. Mencken opened the pages of *American Mercury* to prisoners, and a torrent of manuscripts poured from the prisons and flooded not only the *American Mercury* office, but other magazines as well. The encouragement of the flamboyant Mr. Mencken was all that was needed. Although much of what was produced earned only rejection slips, there were notable exceptions, mainly the work of Ernest Booth and Robert Tasker, both inmates of California prisons. Booth later wrote *Stealing Through Life* and Tasker produced *Grimhaven*.

The autobiographical and "protest" nature of the successful writing in this era brought a public and administrative reaction against it. California adopted stringent censorship for a while in response to the feeling that "convicts are in prison to be punished, not to make money." [3]

But the censorship gave way to permit David Lamson to publish *We Who Are About To Die* as the result of his thirteen months in the death house at San Quentin. Then Caryl Chessman's *Cell 2455 Death Row* in 1954 and *Trial by Ordeal* drew heated debate and considerable public attention to his lengthy ordeal in San Quentin's death row. Ross's *The Dead Are Mine* got favorable reviews in 1963, and in 1966, Frank Elli, a forty-year-old parolee from the Stillwater (Minnesota) prison won a $10,000 award for his first novel, *The Riot*. Scheduled for publication in 1967, Elli's novel was based on his experience in a riot in Walla Walla (Washington) prison. A number of other prison-born novels have also found their way into the literary marketplace, but no established literary personality has yet emerged as a result of writing done in prison.

Literature from behind bars has piqued the curiosity of many for

2. Herman K. Spector, "What Men Write in Prison," *Tomorrow* (December, 1945), pp. 53–56.
3. *Ibid.*

other reasons, too. The standard advice to a novice from professionals and teachers of creative writing is "live life to its fullest—only after experiencing a maximum range of emotional experiences can a person truly be a creative writer." Such advice immediately puts a dash of interest into prison writing because prisoners have had, before and during confinement, extremes of experience that go even beyond the normal fullness of life.

There is no doubt that imprisonment itself must have tremendous impact on the unfortunates who undergo it. What happens to a man's creative spirit when society deposits him behind the gray stone walls and iron gates of a prison? What mental and spiritual torment does imprisonment bring to a person whose sensitivity is greater than most, whose spirit has not yet been dulled or overpowered? Oscar Wilde cried out in hopelessness, "They have taken away my soul; I don't know what they've done with it." [4] Desperately trying to turn adversity into something constructive, he resolved:

> I have got to make everything that has happened to me good for me. The plank bed, the loathsome food, the hard ropes shredded into oakum till one's fingertips grow dull with pain, the menial offices with which each day begins and finishes, the harsh orders that routine seems to necessitate, the dreadful dress that makes sorrow grotesque to look at, the silence, the solitude, the shame—each and all of these things I have to transform into a spiritual experience. [5]

For O. Henry, his caging and subjection to total regimentation constituted the supreme test of endurance that brought him to the brink of suicide. Did this emotional experience have any real effect on his creative ability? His locales and subjects came from earlier, pre-prison experiences or from life in New York later. But what of the writer's ability to observe life's detail so precisely that he can recreate it in words? Or the ability to give dimension to characters that comes from empathy and retrospection? Does imprisonment develop these attributes? There seem to be no pat answers.

Other questions, these of concern to penologists and the public they

4. André Gide, *Oscar Wilde* (New York: Philosophical Library, 1949), pp. 36–37.
5. *Ibid.*, p. 39.

represent, also beg for answers. What good can writing and other creative arts do for the convict? Is writing an aid to rehabilitation? Will the embezzler, the burglar, the kidnapper, the murderer—the so-called common criminal—be more inclined to emerge from prison as a responsible member of society if he has had the opportunity to write for publication while incarcerated?

All of these questions can be answered only with speculation. But the belief that retrospection and self-analysis are essential to rehabilitation is widespread,[6] and these qualities form the fountain from which writing flows. Alex F. Osborn, chairman of the board of the Creative Education Foundation, has indicated that creative imagination can be developed and that it provides the best route to change within a person.[7] In a letter to the editor of Leavenworth's *New Era,* he suggested that rigid conduct patterns can be put aside most easily if the individual develops his creative imagination. Although Mr. Osborn was writing of all creative pursuits, his opinion reflects the thinking of prison administrators who believe in the concept that creative outlets have salutary effects on prisoners.[8]

Support for the thesis that writing is a potential means for developing constructive thought processes has also come from Erle Stanley Gardner. The noted mystery writer has developed a strong interest in the penal press. In his article "The Importance of the Prison Press," Mr. Gardner says:

> . . . writing is about the best way I know to develop insight
> into life and character. You can't write about something without
> studying about it, and when you study the people around you, you
> begin to see beneath the surface. And with each story . . . you

6. The first of three points listed by Lloyd W. McCorkle and Richard R. Korn in "Resocialization within Walls," *Annals of the American Academy of Social and Political Science,* May, 1954, pp. 96–97, is related to this concept. The authors point out that treatment must begin with the person somehow being brought to awareness that his difficulties are related to motives and patterns of perception within himself.

7. Undated letter from Alex F. Osborn to the editor, *New Era,* and published as page 5 of the Summer, 1965, issue of that periodical.

8. Music, drama, painting and other creative arts are also encouraged in most penal institutions. Inmate art shows have attracted considerable attention and have resulted in record sales of paintings in many instances.

gain a little more insight, a little better understanding of life's problems.

Every hour a man spends writing develops his skill and sympathetic perception.[9]

There is no doubt that many prison administrators consider it vital for penal publications to serve as an outlet for creativity. Myrl E. Alexander, director of the federal Bureau of Prisons, has given his endorsement to this aim. It will be recalled (page 50) that this is the most frequently cited goal of the penal press. No other single objective elicited nearly so many positive responses.

A question about the rehabilitative effect of publications work also brought many affirmative responses from administrators. An underlying theme of many of the answers was the constructive effect that self-examination and creative expression could be expected to engender. Some indicated the belief that a noticeable difference in thinking emerged after an inmate had participated in publications work for an extended period.[10]

Inmate editors and writers, in interviews and published comments, have also expressed strong support for the view that self-expression through writing is beneficial. The underlying theme of their comments is that a person must think before he writes, and the unleashing of the thought processes must eventually show the folly of criminal behavior. The resultant pride of accomplishment, ordinarily so lacking in prison life, is also cited. Referring to the non-writing aspects of magazine editing, Al Rutledge of the Maryland *Courier* said: "No man can experience the thrill of starting with blank pages and ending up with an attractive magazine without somehow being a little different as a result."

9. Erle Stanley Gardner, "The Importance of the Prison Press," *Sagebrush* (February, 1958), Nevada State Penitentiary.

10. Some typical responses include: "It allows the inmates an opportunity for self-expression and use of creative abilities that ordinarily would not be available to them" (Hampden County Jail & House of Correction); "Any creative effort over a long period of time is beneficial for the individual or individuals involved" (The *Clock*, Idaho State Penitentiary); "There is a 'thinking' and 'creative' awareness among staff inmates that isn't prevalent among the general population" (The *Insider*, District of Columbia Jail); "It encourages creative and constructive thinking. . . ." (The *Conquerer*, Maryland House of Correction, Jessup.)

In the *Echo* of the Texas Department of Corrections, inmate Jim Campbell related this story:

> . . . We expect a miracle to be accompanied by Divine signs: a star overhead or convulsions of nature. But there are many minor miracles in prison that get no publicity at all.
>
> One such case was a good friend of mine. A man filled with hate if there ever was one. But one day he read a poem that touched him deeply, and filled him with the desire to take up writing poetry himself. Most of his early attempts were awful but in time he sold a few pieces that were really good. Perhaps the greatest profit he obtained, however, had nothing to do with money.
>
> He told me one time, "You know, I never expect to make much money with poetry, but that really doesn't matter. What is important to me is that sometimes I manage to put down a few words on paper that express what I've felt all my life about some one thing. I pull an emotion out of someplace deep down inside me, and when I do I feel as though I'd ripped a chain off my soul." [11]

The intangibles of human nature defy objective measurement. Only the person experiencing a feeling comprehends it completely, and the process of human communication is still not sufficiently precise to convey a feeling with any certainty. Miracles of internal human change can be claimed by some, belittled by others. It is not necessary here to come to any fixed conclusion regarding the *degree* of value that creative writing has for prisoners. The recognition of its having at least a reasonable value by prison officials and inmates is sufficient to merit investigation of the potential outlets for creative writing.

WRITING FOR OUTSIDE PUBLICATIONS

If inmates wish to write for publication, there are two obvious avenues they can take: to outside, free-world publications or to prison-sponsored periodicals.

Writing for commercial publications presents many problems. Quality standards are often beyond a novice's attainment and there conse-

11. Jim Campbell, "Thanksgiving: What Have I To Be Thankful For?" the *Echo* (November, 1964), p. 1.

quently may be little hope for success. Prison officials tend to be skittish about the content of material being sent to mass media. Editors, sometimes victimized in the past, are wary of plagiarism.[12]

An article, written by a convict, in *Saturday Review* illustrates the difficulties of writing for outside publication, but also, by virtue of the fact that it was appearing in a respectable journal, showed that success was possible. The author, Convict No. 49040 (who, by the way, became interested in writing when appointed editor of a prison publication), delineated these difficulties:

> 1. Censorship: [Some states] strangle writing until whatever manuscripts are produced resemble grade-school drivel. . . . Writers are usually allowed to submit manuscripts only to those magazines that appear on an "approved" list.
>
> Generally a manuscript is submitted first to a designated censor (often the prison librarian). . . . If it passes that hurdle, it is forwarded to the associate superintendent or warden. . . . If he, too, approves it, the manuscript is mailed. That is unless you happen to be an inmate in a federal prison or correctional institution. In that case your manuscript must be forwarded to the Bureau of Prisons in Washington. . . .
>
> 2. Supplies: What, for example, does the ordinary writer do when he runs out of manuscript bond, typewriter ribbons, or envelopes? Simple. He makes a quick trip to the stationery store. . . . But for those . . . behind bars, the acquisition of material is somewhat more complex. Prison canteens, which stock a wide variety of toilet articles and edibles, seldom carry the supplies a writer needs. They must be ordered through a special arrangement. . . . It can be quite an ordeal.
>
> 3. Research: The typical prison library is not quite the Library of Congress, and a single missing fact can, as every writer knows, delay an article for months.

12. The *Atlantic*'s Edward Weeks, in a column on plagiarism ("The Peripatetic Reviewer" [January, 1966], p. 115) wrote, "I learned to be wary of manuscripts coming into us from penal institutions. . . . One's instinct is to help, and certainly every editor knows that O. Henry did some of his earliest and best writing while serving time. . . . But for every O. Henry serving time there are a score of prisoners confident that they can fool the world by copying."

4. Facilities: Trying to write in an eight-by-ten cell with an old Rinso carton for a desk, isn't the easiest way to do it.[13]

Other convict writers have belittled the notion that prisoners have abundant spare time for meditation and writing. In most situations, they say, prisoners must put in a normal work day in one of the shops, and fatigue and shortness of time is more of a problem for them than for writers on the outside.

There is no doubt that prison writers have special obstacles to overcome, but these vary greatly among institutions. The personalities of those who are responsible for censorship can make a difference, and the basic outlook of correctional authorities can keep hindrances to a minimum. Two specific cases, both of which have shown unusual literary output from inmates, serve to illustrate.

At San Quentin prison, the librarian must review all manuscripts: books, short stories, poems, feature articles, crossword puzzles, musical compositions, patents, cartoons, inventions, gags, and so forth. The fully trained, professional librarian for several years at San Quentin has been Herman K. Spector, whose enthusiasm for the creative efforts of prisoners has caused him to write on that subject several times. Some of his enthusiasm, and the output generated among San Quentin writers, can be seen in his 1964 report in connection with National Library Week:

> The extent to which our men actively participate in preparing manuscripts . . . and [their] variety are revealed by our cumulative figures which indicated that in sixteen years they have submitted a total of 13,341 such items. . . . This means that every year, on an average, we have cleared for mailing 840 items. . . . We are now awaiting the results of our men's participation in the current HARPERS' MAGAZINE CONTEST. Yes! It's: second prize, third prize, and one honorable mentioned. Three of all seven winners are our men! It's a great victory: their essays will find place within the covers of a century-old magazine, long distinguished for its remarkable editors and the many notable writers. . . .[14]

13. No. 49040, "Writing the Hard Way," *Saturday Review*, September 11, 1965, p. 34.

14. Herman K. Spector, "The Library's Role in the Complex Rehabilitative Programs," National Library Week booklet, 1964, San Quentin Prison, p. 8.

Mr. Spector's report also gives some indication that the hand of censorship is not too heavy: ". . . of the 1198 items which our men contributed this past fiscal period, 88 or 7.3% were rejected by us; 56 or 4.66% were required to be revised, and 953 or 79.40% were approved. . . ." [15]

At Southern Michigan Prison, Jackson, a writing program with unusual inmate responsibility had been in operation for fifteen years before 1966. Portions of a fifteenth anniversary article on the program in the SMP *Spectator* tell of its success and character:

> Fifteen years is a long time for any prison program to operate successfully. But the writer's program here at SMP is celebrating its 15th year of continued success.
>
> Under the supervision of the Department of Treatment, Mr. G. L. Hansen, Director, this program is one of the most rehabilitative, entertaining, educational and profitable pasttimes available to men serving time.
>
> It was started in July, 1951, by former Corrections Commissioner, Earnest C. Brooks, as a "new experiment in modern penology."
>
> Under the "Prison Regulation" formulated to direct the new experiment, three inmates were carefully screened to make up the body of the Manuscript Committee to examine all outgoing material from inmate writers to see that it conformed to institutional regulations. If the material concerned the prison, or if there was any doubt concerning the subject, it was referred to Mr. K. K. Smith, Civilian Manuscript Committee sponsor.
>
> Today the Manuscript Committee operates with four members (another being added as the program expanded) . . . Robert Tate is assigned to the office on a full time paid basis.
>
> "Free-lance writing privileges are open to anyone interested in developing his creative writing ability, making the best use of this institution's treatment facilities," said Mr. Hansen.
>
> "Probably the biggest problem that confronts the prison writer," stated Mr. K. K. Smith, "is research. Whereas a writer in the free-world might just pick up a telephone and get the information he needs, the incarcerated writer has to really dig. In most cases the writer can write to various concerns outside and get his data.

15. *Ibid.*

But this in itself can hurt the sale of an article, especially when timeliness is involved."

According to Tate, nearly four-hundred manuscripts leave the prison monthly. And over three hundred editors have responded with checks.

Probably the "hottest" selling writer at SMP is Pete Simer, who works in the Upjohn Clinic. Simer started writing about three and a half years ago. He got lucky with an article entitled "Nobody Votes In My Town." To date Simer has sold the piece over three-hundred times to non-conflicting markets for a total of over $8,000.

Another writer, Hugh "Buzz" Dillon, was named an editorial associate of *Freelance*, an outside writer's magazine.

"In my opinion, the experiment has been a complete success," said Gus Harrison, Corrections Director. "The cost is very nominal. This gives inmates an opportunity to find expression for any creative ability they may have. From the point of re-socializing prisoners, no one can definitely state the potential." [16]

Sensible writing programs can produce a reasonable amount of success for the writers in any correctional institution. Contests especially for writers in confinement are helpful, too. And there always will be a limited market for articles on prison subjects that only inmates can properly handle. But on the whole, the real hope for publication of prisoner-written material rests with inmate-edited periodicals.

CREATIVE EXPRESSION IN PRISON PERIODICALS

The case for inmate periodicals as the most feasible outlets for convict writing rests basically on four points. Perhaps most important is the fact that there is room in these periodicals for novices' efforts. The tyro has virtually no chance of seeing his work published in outside periodicals; his chances with his institution's publication are usually good. Many publication supervisors such as Miss Marguerite Givens of the Federal Reformatory for Women in Alderson, West Virginia, commit their periodicals to a definite policy of encouraging

16. Clay O'Droske, "SMP Writing Program Celebrating 15th Year," the *Spectator*, February 18, 1966, p. 3.

beginning writers. Miss Givens lets the amount of material submitted be the prime determinant of the size of each issue of the *Eagle* so that even the more amateurish material can be included.

Publication of his earliest material is encouragement of the strongest kind for the novice writer. The assurance that he has an outlet for his material often is the deciding factor in getting him to finish a piece of writing.

A third advantage of the inmate periodical is its ability to accept a broader range of material from its writers. Most prison writing in outside publications is about the prisoner's incarceration; only with such subjects does he have an advantage over other writers. When writing for a prison publication, however, inmates can do essays, poems, short stories, editorials, and feature articles that would not be of interest to an outside market. The almost limitless range of subjects and types of writing for prison magazines and newspapers provides much more valuable experience.

Lastly, although it is difficult to explain or justify, prison administrators seem to be much more lenient with the censorship of material intended for inmate magazines than for outgoing writing. This broader freedom of expression also tends to make prison-produced periodicals especially valuable as outlets for self-expression.

QUALITY AND CONTENT OF INMATE WRITING

Much of the content of penal publications is of a news nature: sports, bloodmobile visits, parole board appearances, population statistics, and the like (see Chapter 4). Here we shall be concerned with what would be considered, in a general sense, as literary material: essays, poetry, and fiction.

Some conclusions stand out as a result of a review of prison-born literature, including books past and present, material in outside periodicals, and the content of prison magazines and newspapers. The idea that prison is a breeding place for literary genius seems to be a myth fostered hopefully by the writers now behind bars and by others aware of the great literature produced in confinement. Aside from William Sidney Porter's contributions, there is very little to support this thesis.

The great literature from prisons came from men who were articulate, who had the stamp of greatness upon them as a *cause* for their confinement. Most other works have tended to be autobiographical discourses that got public attention because of the prisoner's circumstance and not his contribution to literature. Modern prison writers agree that prison is not an ideal place for writing; its psychological and physical disadvantages far outweigh any advantages.

These comments are by no means intended to minimize or detract from the importance of writing for prisoners; the value of writing, for the writer, is not dependent upon the lasting quality of his output. Nor are these observations intended to imply that prison publications should not be given maximum encouragement as an outlet for literary expression. The increased use and improved status of prison magazines represent the best hope for stimulating a larger and more worthwhile output of inmate writing. Their value as a source of lasting literature in the future and as a stimulant to constructive thinking on the part of their editors and contributors is beyond question.

How good has the content of prison magazines been? What do prisoners write about? In most respects, the literary content has been what anyone would expect. A wide range of educational and environmental backgrounds is reflected in the quality, which ranges from semi-literate to excellent. Subject matter is strongly influenced by background and the prison environment. Essays on penology are common. So are articles on legal problems. "Time" is a favorite subject. Poetry is abundant, for although poetry represents a rather small percentage of space, it accounts for greater numbers of contributors than prose does. Fiction is often apparently autobiographically inspired; "cops and robbers" subjects predominate, but there is also a tendency to concentrate on sentimental subjects such as home and family. Christmas never fails to produce outbursts of sentimentality, but there is bitterness, too. To an outsider, perhaps the most striking aspect of content is the humorous material that finds its way into prison magazines. One's sense of humor seems to be able to withstand the disadvantages of confinement.

Only by reading some of the literary output of prison writers can an outsider get a realistic view—a "feel"—of the literary content of prison publications. With that in mind, some representative selections are presented here. No attempt has been made to correct spelling, capitalization, and other mechanics of style. These are representative of the better material, but are not intended to show only the best; in terms of content and quality many other items not included are as good and as typical as these.

Jack Hollon's version of "Jack & the Beanstalk" is an example of the jargon and the humorous outlook of many prison writers; "Kings, Ichthyologists, and Fish Ponds," "How Do I Stay Out of Penitentiaries?" and "My Dungeon Shook" are typical of the thought pieces on the subjects of penology and prisoner rehabilitation. "Flop House" represents the many articles and stories on what could have been personal background; Ken Wesley's "Time Is A River" was widely reprinted in the penal press and represents the many discussions of time and its meaning. "Sister of the Brave" and "Her Lawn Canopy" were selected to show the fiction of a general, "outside world" nature. Christmas sentiment is represented by Jack Leighton's " 'Tis Christmas." The poetry and short selections are primarily on prison-related thoughts and feelings; other subjects are treated by prison poets, but they seem mainly to feel the need to express ideas about confinement and its effects on them.

Selected Writings of Inmates

The TRUE Story of Jack & the Beanstalk

JACK HOLLON

ONCE UPON A TIME there was a young man who, through an unfortunate accident that one day happened to his Father, was left as the sole support of his Mother. Now this young fellow was a fine upstanding citizen and a credit to the community in which he lived, but he was a little short in the brain department and was finding it hard to make ends meet. One day he woke up bright and early to find his Mother weeping in the kitchen. Son, she tells him, it looks like the end has about got here. We are out of everything and you know that I can't stand this milk all the time so take the cow to town and see if you can sell her and get us some goodies. Don't forget the Tokay, either.

So Jack like the good son that he was, went out to the pasture and slapped a bridle on old Bossy and took off for town and the local stockyards.

Going down the road he met a fellow and stopped to find out the latest news. Now this fellow, an old geezer, sized up Jack and seeing that he was not the brightest boy in the world figured that he could beat him for the cow. Look boy, he tells him, I sure hope that you are not going to try to sell that cow in town. Why the market has went bad on cattle and they are almost giving them away today. This little statement shook our Hero up no end and he says what am I going to do? My poor Old Mother is about to starve to death and worse than that she is out of wine and this milk is about to do her in. The old sharpie seeing that he has the fish hooked good, says, lookie here son, I have with me some magic beans and with them you don't have to ever worry about food again, they will grow anything and what you don't need yourself you can sell and get your Mom all the wine she can drink. Jack says, Boy, that's just what I need. How much do you want for them. Well, son, says the old man, tell you what I will do. Seeing as how your old Mother is about to starve to death I'll just trade you for that worthless cow that you have got. Good deal, Cries Jack and makes the trade. The old man quick grabs the cow and takes off for town and

115

a good time and Jack heads for home to tell his Mom all about the good deal that he made.

Now when Jack hits the door the first thing that his poor feeble old Mother says is, you didn't forget the Tokay, did you son? Well, Mom, Jack says, and proceeds to give her a rundown on the good trade that he made and how she will soon have all the wine that she can drink. The old lady not being a lame brain like her son blows her top and tottering over to him proceeds to pick him up and toss him and the bag of beans out the window without bothering to open it.

After the old lady went to sleep Jack figured that it was safe to go back in the house, so leaving the beans where they were he snuck in and went to bed hoping that the old lady would cool down by morning. First thing next day the old lady is screaming in his ear, get up you lazy Jack—and go get rid of the tree that is growing outside the window. Jack goes out and looks and sure enough there is this tree growing clear up out of sight. Now Jack being a curious fellow decided to climb up and see how far the tree really went. Climbing all day he finally gets to the top of it and starts to look around. Off in the distance he spies some thing that looks like a house and wondering who would live clear up here he goes to investigate. He gets to the house and going in he sees this Giant sitting on a chair playing with a goose. Now Jack almost lost his uppers when the Giant tells this goose, lay or in the pot you go and the goose lays a big golden egg. But even though Jack's a real nut he can see that is a better deal than a sack of beans so he starts to figure how he could get the goose. Well, luck is with him as the Giant after making the goose lay a couple more eggs falls asleep. Jack right away runs in and puts the snatch on the goose and makes it for the tree. Now this goose not knowing Jack starts to scream stop thief, put me down, help Police and all that kind of stuff. All this commotion wakes up the Giant and he takes off after Jack full blast. Well, our Hero is no slouch and he gets to the tree and is half way down it before the Giant gets out of the house. Getting to the bottom he grabs an axe and starts chopping away and not a minute too soon either as the Giant and the tree hit the ground together and I guess you know that the sudden stop puts the Giant out of commission. Seeing that he don't have to worry about him Jack slowly saunters in the house, and says look Mom what I got. You don't have to join A. A. now. The old lady seeing nothing but a goose is about to throw him out again when Jack says to the bird, man, get with it or in the pot you go. Bingo, the fowl comes out with a solid gold egg. At this shot the old lady's eyes light up and she forgives Jack for being such a beetlebrain. Now the old lady not knowing when all this will end keeps the goose busy all day knocking out eggs and when she has a barn full of them, off to town she goes not to buy a jug of Tokay as you might think, but the whole winery.

Now everything is going smooth for a few days and the old gal is really living it up and Jack isn't doing too bad himself, when there comes a knock on the door one morning. When the old lady opens the door the fellow standing there flashes a badge and tells her, I'm from the Internal Revenue Service and I would like to talk to this guy named Jack. What about, says the old lady. Well, this fellow says, we got a report from one of your neighbors that a couple weeks ago Jack didn't even have a pot to put the milk in and now he is making the scene like John D. and we want our tax money. Well, the old lady makes a deal with him so that she won't lose the winery and tells him that Jack is down to the local pool hall. The IRS man calls the sheriff and down to the pool hall they go and put the arm on poor Jack for income tax evasion. Well, Jack as big a fool as they come, tells them all about the goose and the golden eggs and has him knock out a few to pay the taxes. This makes the IRS man happy but the sheriff wants to know where he got the goose and Jack like an idiot tells him all about the Giant and how he got him from the Giant and how he had to chop the tree down to save his life. Well, the sheriff goes out to Jack's place and digs up the body and quick as a flash he arrests him and charges him with Grand Larceny and Murder and to top it off they confiscate the goose for evidence. Well to cut a long story short, poor old Jack got the chair when his Mother turned states evidence and the goose died from overwork when the Government tried to get him to lay enough eggs to pay off the National Debt. The only one that came out of the deal with anything was Jack's Mother. She got to keep the winery and not being a lame like Jack she had several eggs stashed away for her old age and never ran off the mouth about them to anyone.

There is a moral to this story and that's this: if you are left to support your Mother don't sell the cow for beans. Go to the unemployment office and get Mom a job scrubbing floors or something, and whatever you do, pay your TAXES!

(Reprinted from the *Recount*, Vol. 8, Nos. 2 & 3, Summer–Fall, 1963, Colorado State Penitentiary.)

"NOTIFY THE 'NEW ERA' TO CANCEL MY SUBSCRIPTION"

William Drummond, *New Era* (promotional material, n.d.; U.S. Penitentiary, Leavenworth)

Kings, Ichthyologists, and Fish Ponds

Jim Fritz

ONCE UPON A TIME in the Greatest Country in the world—during the Time of Yesterday, and on the vast estate of the willing, but incapable, King Nescience—was located a beautiful and spacious garden. This garden was a veritable cornucopia of vegetation and abundance. Growing therein was a countless variety of flowers, plants, and trees, ranging from the stately Redwood tree thru the lowly but fruitful potato vine. It was a wonderful garden and everyone seeing it could hardly help but compare it with the fabled Garden of Eden.

Now in this garden, situated almost in the exact center of it, was a large and ornate Fish Pond. Herein, at all hours of the day and night, swimming busily around—frolicing, diving, gliding, and enjoying the cool, clear essence of the water—were millions upon millions of multi-colored fish. A chance visitor stumbling on this idyllic water scene would be immediately charmed by the aquatic aura of harmony which seemed to exist in this beautiful and sparkling panorama—was his attention not drawn to isolated instances of non-conformity amongst the silvery-finned denizens. Here and there, if the visitor was a skilled observer, he could single out certain strangely acting fish which were evidently not contributing to the mellifluous motion of the majority, but seemed to be obstinately darting hither and yon in direct conflict to the stream of the many. This, in contrast to the goal of most of the fish (which—upon careful study of their movements, passage, and destination—seemed to be a continuous circling of their watery confines in a never-ending journey), was enough to interrupt, inconvenience, and impede their seemingly perpetual progress. If the visitor would have tarried long enough to witness the feeding hour he would have found much more evidence of non-conformity in the actions of these rebel fish.

Each evening at sundown, small, pipelike mechanisms at the north end of the pond would swing into motion and as each fish passed them they would eject a certain amount of food. This continued until the greater number of the fish had been fed, and then the feeding stations (for this is what the pipelike mechanisms were) abruptly halted their

119

dispensing of food. Then, if the observer would have calculated the number of fish remaining unfed, he would probably have found to his astonishment that they added up to exactly the number of rebel fish he had seen earlier attempt to disrupt the harmonious flow of conforming fish painstakingly making their foreordained rounds. Naturally he would have automatically reached the conclusion that the amount of food dispensed was in direct proportion to the number of fish in the pond and the number of trips they had earlier made past these feeding stations. He would have been correct in his conclusion, for that is exactly the mechanized method by which these fish were fed each day.

Of course this would have been a very practical and labor-saving method of provisioning these delightfully formed and beautifully colored fish if the Ichthyologist appointed by the king had been painstaking enough in his original observation of their ichthyological habits to realize that in every school of fish there are non-conformists—or odd balls. But instead of observing and experimenting with a large enough group so that he could reach a true conclusion, he was invariably lazy and hasty, and had satisfied himself with insufficient data.

But what of the fish who were left unfed each day? In this group by odds of chance were both those who had conformed to the majority's intentions of each contributing his expected number of rounds so that all would be fed, and the rebels who evidently didn't give a damn if some of their contemporaries were unfairly deprived or not. Imagine the surprise and the poor sucker-like looks on the faces of the innocent fish that first day when they finally realized their day's swimming was for naught. No wonder it was not long before the rebels were ostracized and looked down upon.

And in the days that followed it was only appropriate that the conforming fish, by sheer strength of numbers, insured that the recalcitrant and rebellious fish were usually last in the stream of lines leading to the feeding stations. Eventually this led to the rebel fish exercising every strategem they could—short of swimming the expected rounds for feeding—to pilfer, sponge, steal, and hi-jack from their earning brethren. (Sound familiar?)

There soon came to be such a turmoil in the once quiet and congruous Fish Pond that it wasn't long before King Nescience was informed of this. Shocked and angered at the audacity of the rebel fish in even daring to disrupt any regal procedure that he had ordained, he ordered a smaller, separate fish pond to be built in the exact center of the larger one, its walls to be constructed of solid rock in order that no one (not even the other fish) could see inside, and he decreed that all recalcitrant and rebel fish be transferred therein immediately. And he designated the official Ichthyologist (the lazy, hasty one who had failed in his original observation of the fish) to use any and all methods of punishment he thought necessary to break the spirit of the rebel fish.

Being sadistic by nature, the Ichthyologist immediately set to work with relish. He starved the rebel fish, he beat them, he flayed them, he hung them up by their gills, he isolated some of them in the underwater channels of the new fish pond (which, by the way, was soon mockingly called the "Clink"). Some of the hardier and more troublesome rebels he put to death by flipping them out of their watery prison and on to the large rock on the small island in the center of the pond where they slowly and agonizingly died under the hot midday sun. (This form of punishment was officially called Dehydration, but was soon appropriately referred to by the rebel fish as "getting the 'hot rock' ").

After varying periods of time, the rebel fish who were still alive (the ones who hadn't gone "stare crazy": symptom of such was subject continually and lifelessly swimming indolently around and around in a one or two foot circle and exhibiting two large, staring pop-eyes) were returned to the outer confines of the Fish Pond. But after a short period of time, a large percentage of them were up to their old tricks —so it was back to the "Clink" again, over and over in a never-ending cycle.

The years passed by in this Greatest Country in the world with the problem of the Fish Pond and the rebel fish still not solved. Finally, in the Time of Today, there succeeded to the throne a more learned and modern king who was given the name of King Inexpedience. Immediately on his coronation, he decided he would solve the problem of the Fish Pond and the rebel fish without delay. Wasting no time, he hurriedly fired the current Ichthyologist (who was of the same mold as the one of King Nescience's reign) and hired a new one who was reputed to have had remarkable success throughout the world with his daring, new and unheard of, Ichthyological theories.

This new Ichthyologist had worked with fish for such a great length of time that he had a lot of compassion even for the rebel fish, and it was said that he occasionally identified with them. But whether or not this is true, it must be stated that he attempted with all his skill and resources to not only punish the rebel fish as had his predecessors done, but to actually try to rehabilitate them. Though he still confined the rebel fish to the "Clink" he went so far as to change the stone walls of this inner fish pond to walls of glass whereby the rebels could look out at the world outside, and their more conforming brethren look in. He did away with all forms of corporal punishment, closed the under-water isolation channels, didn't starve the rebel fish (in fact he fed them almost as good as the slower swimming conforming fish were fed on the outside), didn't use the "Rock" on the small island in the center of the "Clink," and did all within his power to see, that once the rebel fish were returned to the larger Fish Pond, they would conform and swim on their way, lawfully earning their right to live in this freer society.

And actually this new Ichthyologist had a fair measure of success. But alas, like his predecessors, he still didn't seem to fully realize that each of these rebel fish was a complete individual needing separate and different treatment in order to disclose the basic individual problems involved that governed his unexplainable conduct. And so, due to this and to the fact that he didn't have sufficient assistance and available facilities, and because of the tight purse strings of the well-meaning but miserly King Inexpedience, he was doomed to failure at the start. Again a goodly number of rebel fish entered and exited the "Clink" with the frequency of a yo-yo moving to and fro on its string.

So, of course, more years passed until the Time of Tomorrow rolled around. Kings and Ichthyologists came and went with the regularity of the seasons. And then one day there succeeded to the throne a young and handsome king with a shock of wavy, unruly hair—a great grand-son of King Nekkedy who had reigned a span of years before—and who was rightfully given the name of King Percipience. From child-hood he had studied all available data on the ever-enlarging Fish Pond with its growing number of rebel fish and the problems they presented, and he had made a vow that if he ever inherited his great grandfather's throne he would succeed in solving the problem regardless of the expense. He was a sagacious and gracious sovereign, and he realized that the problem was of paramount importance. Knowing this, he immediately channeled funds—funds that had been year after year tossed away on such costly projects as Aid to Lower Slobovia, Lend-Lease to Outer Gonmolia, and the audacious and hare-brained idea of sending a rocket to Heaven containing an envoy who would petition the Deity in an attempt to absolve the people's feelings of guilt—and made them available for use in solving the immediate problems at hand. (He was the type of an individual who would clean out his own castle BEFORE advising a neighboring king to do the same.) He appointed not one or two or three—but a score of the ablest Ichthyologists in the world and set them to work. Then he acquired a multitude of minor assistants to aid these learned men in giving the rebel fish the individual diagnosis and treatment that was needed. He tore down the walls of the "Clink" and built another Fish Pond adjacent to the original, and equipped it exactly like the first, except that he added diagnosing pools, class-room pools, and treatment pools in which the questions of "How? Why? and Wherefore?" were given prime importance. It no longer was: "Do this or else!!" But became: "Do this this way or that way because of this reason or that reason." Emphasis was placed on finding out why the rebel fish reacted the way they did, and it was painstakingly explained and taught them—through easily learned conditioning—the vast satisfaction the rebel fish would reap by conforming to the pattern of living that had been ordained for them. And through it all they were instructed and aided in the methods by which they could succeed in living a fruitful and beneficial life.

They came to realize that they had somehow acquired the wrong values during their formative years, and they were all shown exactly where and why they had gone off on a tangent.

And finally coming to understand this, they accepted it; and when they were returned to their beloved old Fish Pond, they willingly and congenially earned their food by swimming their days away in the Stream of Life.

(Reprinted from the *Terrescope*, Vol. V, No. 24, November 6, 1964, United States Penitentiary, Terre Haute, Indiana.)

How Do I Stay Out of Penitentiaries?

ROBERT PRESTON

A Dialogue

A: How do I stay out of penitentiaries?

B: Quit stealing.

A: Very original.

B: Stop committing crimes.

A: How did you ever figure it out?

B: Pretty easy to figure it out. Difficult to admit it.

A: That begs the question.

B: And the question?

A: The question is how do I quit stealing? I have strong desires, compulsions, obsessions, neuroses, needs, a bad temper, a bad work record, a bad criminal record, and so on. It's pretty simple to say, "Quit stealing," but that doesn't impress me much. Then too I am stubborn, I still think that given the right opportunity and all, I can beat them. Furthermore, I am a rebel at heart and want revenge, son, revenge. I'm a mess of strong contradictions and impulses and deep passionate feelings. It's a complex thing and you give me a simple (and I might add a very corny) answer.

B: How do you quit stealing? First, you've got to want to, or else you have to be bone-tired of getting caught all the time and have reached the self-esteem-shattering conclusion that you are just too ignorant and stupid to commit crimes and get away with them, because of innate lack of subtlety and powers of organization and planning and caution and perception, not to mention the spotlighting effect of your past record, etc. In other words, one way or another, you have to be about half wise to yourself, wise to the unflattering facts involved in your little old case, your special, unique little old personality, which is so very very different from everyone else's on this spinning globe.

A: You sound bitter, man.

B: I am bitter, against self-ignorance and stupidity, especially my own.

124

A: Proceed. Let's say I want to do all this, that I'm wise to all this. What do I *do?*

B: Practice restraint. Not know what it is: *practice* it. In little things: Don't butt in on people's conversations, hold back in chow lines, commissary lines and movie lines, don't give in to your impulses so quickly, make little sacrifices. A river unchecked runs to many places where it does no good, but a dam (my symbol of restraint) allows man to *control* the uses of the flowing water. And even the water backed up is used for power, it's pressure being channeled effectively into power in reserve. It's a law of nature, and like all laws, it cannot be broken. You change a law or you neglect a law; but you do not break a law. A law will break you, but you will not break a law, especially a law of nature. And it is a law of nature, this restraint-is-necessary-for-self-control axiom. Many people think that when a thing comes up in the future they will somehow be ready for it without preparation. They say things such as, "That's all right. When the time comes I'll be ready. If I set my mind to do something, I can do it. You can believe that." Well, I don't believe it. It is hot air. It is fantasy, especially if the thing to be done is very difficult, major, or significant. *Practice.* Knowledge is not enough. Practice, a gradual preparation in a new type response to life's experience. Rex Warner said that all civilization depended upon restraint. A point worth pondering.

A: And this will keep me out of penitentiaries?

B: It will help, if you practice it. Find little ways of your own to honestly practice restraint and self-control, and know once and for all that pledges, resolves, resolutions, promises, vows and all such things will never do the job. One must practice now acting the way he knows he must act in critical situations that may come up in the future. You do not tell yourself you are going to do something; you start doing it now, start acting gradually in similar ways and get wise to unpleasantness and discomfort and sacrifice, all the old-fashioned corny things that will be new and fresh when we are all dead and gone because they are in the very texture of the way things are, nature. We must get in touch with this reality or we will waste our lives in fantasy and frustration and hopeless plans all our lives. And such wisdom (in the doing of it) is the wisdom of all artists and saints and scientists and of anyone who has ever accomplished anything in life which is significant. It will help you do anything better, and as a matter of fact you can't really do much without it.

A: What about stealing?

B: Yes, even that. You can misuse truth in many ways. Restraint. Restraint not for the sake of restraint, remember; but restraint for the sake of control, self-control, so that your intellect can have some say in determining what you do and what you don't do, instead of you simply being the slave of your emotions and the world's (and your own) every impulse and caprice and haphazard and dangerous and wrongheaded desire momentarily pleasant and fulfilling perhaps but ultimately destructive and frustrating and defeating.

A: This all sounds very well, something like what Krosen said: "The obsessions of the paranoid are the truths of tomorrow." And I honestly sense that there is a great truth in what you say, and yet . . . and yet . . . well, I don't know . . .

B: It's do or don't. You have free will, so you must choose. All good things are hard come by: surely you've learned *that much* from experience? As your own life proves, and as does mine and most everyone else around here, the old easy saw about experience being the best teacher is mostly a lot of hot air because it only tells half the story. Experience *is* the best teacher, no doubt about it. But man is a very poor student, a bad learner. But as I say, surely you know that good things are hard to come by—that is, good things *to keep*.

A: Yes, that's true. But what about that long hard grind?

B: I know what you mean. Practicing asceticism (restraint, self-denial, self-control, etc.) will help you tough it out. That much should be obvious: only a fool flies in the face of his best hard-earned wisdom. Then too, the reserve and the other good qualities of character which emanate from such practice will make you more alert to the real opportunities with which you will come in contact along the way—along the long hard-grinding way of toughing it out with reality, the way things really are. To neglect these truths is to have a loser going; to incorporate them into your outlook, your vision of life, to make them part of your honest response to experience: this is to have a winner going. Stop always taking the easy way out.

A: Man, are you kidding, or what?

B: No, I'm serious. You never really find out who you are until you get involved with some of these necessary self-disciplines, you never really explore yourself and therefore you cannot exploit the best that is in you, you do not ever discover the depths and breadths of who you are, you are really only living with a very small surface bit of your true potential. Tighten up on your own integrity.

A: All right, all right. I'll think about it.

B: That won't help much. Try some of it, do some of it, don't just think about it.

A: A man's denied enough things in here as it is.

B: That doesn't count because it is forced upon you. It is the spiritual strength that comes from *self*-denial that I am talking about. You've heard the common saying, "You've got to give up something," haven't you.

A: Yes.

B: Well, it's basically the same principle. But why labor the point. Just try it and get wise to what is really happening in life and quit cheating yourself out of its deep richness and meaning.

A: I'll try it out maybe . . . when I get back on the streets, when I get back in the free world.

B: Wrong. *All* the world is free. Do it now. For instance, what kind of pie are we having tonight?

A: Banana cream—my favorite.

B: Your favorite pie?

A: Yes.

B: Good. Give it away—to someone you don't know, with no thought of getting anything in return and see how it makes you feel. Just check your complex of emotions, study the feeling closely. Experiment.

A: Man, you got to be crazy! Why should I give up a piece of my favorite pie to a chump I don't even know?

B: It'll help you stay out of penitentiaries.

A: I can just see myself doing that.

B: And what kind of light cord have you got in your cell?

A: A long one that reaches right down to my bed so I can turn it on and off easily.

B: Cut it off so short that you'll have to stand on tiptoe every time you turn it on or off. And similar things of your own choosing.

A: Man, get on away from me! Are you crazy?

B: A little, I suppose.

A: Do *you* do things like that?

B: Not as often as I should, and then sometimes when I do, I feel all proud or self-righteous, which is all wrong and phony, but I go right ahead because I know that I'm going in the right direction. A few experiences and you know this is the right direction because you start getting real answers as you move along with your doubts and fears in your individual solitude. Well, anyway, you wanted to know—

A: Yeah. How to stay out of penitentiaries.

B: Quit stealing. That is *how*. Now you know. But my point is that it is not enough to know.

A: I got to give up my banana cream pie?

B: In a manner of speaking.

A: Yeah, but what about environment, childhood influences and all that.

B: There are some good things to learn from studying such sociology, but in my opinion, this will probably do you little good. Once again, it is knowledge, and knowledge is not enough. Eventually, if you look long enough, meditate long enough, sum up your experience with an unflattering and tough-minded analysis, you will find that it all comes back around to what I am trying to say, or, more properly, what I am trying to suggest.

A: I know. That I got to give up my banana cream pie.

B: Something like that, yes.

(Reprinted from *New Era*, Summer, 1964, United States Penitentiary, Leavenworth, Kansas.)

My Dungeon Shook

JAMIE BOYCE

PROLOGUE

There was a letter from home today . . . the usual lines. Reba did, interestingly enough, note that little Johnny had made his first trip to the dentist and had responded with far more equanimity than she does in the same situation. A seven year old to the dentist, I pondered aloud? Don't the local five and dime stores sell that rugged cotton known as twine anymore? That string used to have a two-fold purpose around the home: to fly a boy's kite, and to pull his milk-teeth. Also, I wondered if a boy in these times proudly perambulates from the dentist chair holding that first real magnificent manifestation in his hand, then carefully places it under his pillow in the evening; and if the fairy-godfather still calls during the night and leaves a shiny dime in exchange for the tooth? Oh well, times do change, and so do traditions. Gee, how I wish I could see little Johnny this evening.

DEAR FRIEND MEILICHIOS:*

Reflections of Reba and little Johnny, and others, who are solicitous of my welfare, set off a chemical chain of soul searching thoughts that distended all the way to the dark dungeon inside me where there lurks an insatiable desire to challenge the mores of my community. Also, I write this because you are the god of my world—whether I like my world or not—and have far more understanding and commisseration with what I have to say and feel than others who have only a tepid interest in my well-being.

I need deliverance, Meilichios, not necessarily mere liberation from these cells, and walls, and fences. I need to be set free from the concupiscence of nothingness; from that strong desire for material gains and false stimulations that so dominated my being in the outside world. Nothingness. My swift dashes in that rat race thing—running for nothing as a member of that team that trains on greed and evil—has left me with a vacuum of aloneness.

* Editor's Note: Meilichios, in Greek mythology, is Zeus—as a god who is the custodian of the underworld. [This editor's note is by the prison author.]

Tacitly you have shared these vapid hours with me, these hours of aloneness—separate—egregious. This loneliness, which slowly inundates my sleeping quarters each evening before lights are out, is a narration, florid, hard to touch; a narrative that is recounted from somewhere, or from someone, and overwhelms me with an exigent need to face the issue. I have got to have a restorative. Why then, at nights, do I regress to that escape hatch known as somnolence—rather than answer the call to put forth the entire amount at one time? Sleep is no tranquilizer. Sleep does not obviate this remarkably bad narration, obviously, because the same pains of aloneness are with me when I grope along the edge of my bed for my slippers each morning.

Now then, where might I find restorative solutions to ease—just a bit—my nightly pains? Is fear a contributor to my loneliness? I do walk among convicts with deep senses of trepidation because there hangs above my head, like the sword of Damocles, the images of savagery and disease that I see in them. I know that the con who is my friend this moment might brutally assault my person in the next immediate seconds, simply because we argued over which is the better brand of cigarettes. Further, I am aware that while walking down a corridor, or on a range, a little pack of convicts might spring from anyplace, and attack like commandos, simply because there was disagreement over whether or not the ball hit the net in a game of ping pong—last week. Intense fear has a million faces, but the anxieties I suffer most are my fears that my psyche will decay to a point where I am one of the above concerned.

Yes, I would catalogue fear as a factor; and lying too. This dislike for convicts is even more apparent when I walk the corridors and yard, sit over coffee, or lean against the shaded side of a building and hear tales of oppulence and control of meretricious distaffs, from lying convicts. Granted an iota of truth is in some tales of wealth, and whores, and happiness, they are still liars, because they are lying to themselves. Bliss has a sort of pilot light in perpetuity; something that one can reach up from the dark dungeon of his soul—when in his aloneness—and touch. These lies touch nothing except the real insecurity of the men regaling upon them.

From somewhere, I hear that old old voice of someone tell me that the solution must include—in addition to fear and lies—the intricate chemical mixture of guilt. That old voice of the narration serenely whispers to me . . . "If a man feels no guilt, none at all—then he feels no loneliness." Period.

Guilt? Where might I look in search of this compound? I should like to hurry and drink the libation which holds the promise of peace for my soul. I have considered the point and find it incredulous that within penance I should find a solution for acts repugnant to the minions of society; because I feel no remorse for the overt acts perpetrated, or conspiracy, or whatever, as alleged by the authorities of the law. All that I find in a call to action before a judge and jury is a summon to answer to Exodus 20:12–17; and with possible exception to the sale and use of narcotics, the Ten Commandments, I surmise, do encompass all that appears in center stage courtroom dramas. Which means, in reality, that the 20th Century Society I live in is standardized by the 1512 B.C. law of Moses, or Hammarubi ("An eye for an eye . . ."), and if the awareness of those two, since childhood, did nothing for my conscience and the dark dungeon which permeates this separateness throughout my soul, what can an angelic judge and jury accomplish in their so-called findings of facts—under our present rules—except a statistic?

What is gained for me, or society (considering pleas of guilt before them) when words of remorse and humility are spoken, but not felt? Only a mere bureau statistic!

Not being able to find my guilt or solutions for my separateness and aloneness in the above, I suppose I should next move the clinical investigation to my free world environment. Funny, my entrails crawl when I recount the frolic and apparent togetherness once shared with my fellow adventurers on the outside, because I see in them the same despicable lot that I see in penitentiary inmates. Careful cogitation with this similitude is assessed in the tiny capsule of the true values my partners and I had for one another when that steel door joined in marriage with concrete slabs—so to speak—to hold us amenable for our alleged acts. Our orbit in togetherness had been a ruse, deceiving to the actual picture of our distrust for one another; our comaraderie was nothing but the artifice of "self-hypnosis." It allowed us to blind ourselves to what one actually saw in the other: greed—and evil and guilt—and a decaying weakness where use of narcotics was concerned. This must obviously be so, because we told on one another—to those very same minions of the law we had previously "crossed pinkies" and vowed, never!—and throughout all the giving of information, we managed not to countenance the truth of our individual exploits and miscreant efforts (most of which the law knows nothing about.) Alas! Pity, because in facing the truth, I would have seen that the abhorrence I felt for my finking fellow adventurers in its precise image, was a subterfuge of the fear I had of exposing the greed and weakness of someone I thought I knew very well, Myself!

Myself? Are the compounds for the solutions to this loneliness I feel so relatively near? When I pause to muse over the immediate questions, it appears that my thoughts have been contrary to what my ego seeks to manifest. Fear and lying and guilt produce strange enzymes when mixed into the cytoplasm of myself, but let me swallow the libation of my new found discovery. I now see that the truculent faces in the convict crowd—99 and 44/100 percent of whom I neither like nor trust—and the morbidly sad minds I have adjudged as being without understanding and love for anything except the saturnine self, is an image of me; because I walk among them not as a name, but as a number!

I am one of those contemptible bureau statistics! No matter how much scorn I have for courts and juries and their system of cops and hacks, and no matter the amount of my contempt for underworld characters, the irradiating fact is that because of my greed, and guilt and evil—I am a mark in the system.

How sweet it would be if I could blame a minute portion of my aloneness on my comrades and fraternal associates in crime, or on the judge and jury, or the minions of the law—but I cannot. I would only glorify my status as a lying convict (I do my share of Cadillac driving and money counting, etc.) and the magic solution in my discovery, plus the old old voice of the narration, combine to send home this allegory: My lying tongue by day serves only as a booster for my loneliness by night; because my tales, although true at times, are impalpable. I am presently aware that if it were possible, in truth, I would trade all of those glorious moments shared in crime, or as the result of criminal activity, if tonight I could exchange those memories for the touch of a 'snaggled tooth' little boy and witness his slightly withdrawn "Hello."

The upshot is—if I am to be liberated from my loneliness—I must disassociate myself from crime and the fraternal association with the people of that part of the world which is your domain, Meilichios. I need not preclude my contempt for any part of the system which put me here, and holds me, but I will have to keep clear of all paths that lead in the direction of that system (and I am able to recognize them, you can be sure of that.) Too, I must forget about my outside image—which never did exist anyway—and I have to live a life of self-abnegation and humility.

EPILOGUE:

It is indeed odd how so many moments of truth can be lived through reflections of a boy's extracted tooth (I mean, like an analogy to crime and punishment and de-institutionalization.) It came to me that little Johnny, at seven, is in what the behavioral scientists term the 'latent' stage. Like so, I was undeveloped in crime. The milk tooth—to explore a point—is the first organ in the body to manifest itself; by pain, and then by unshackling. True, nature will replace that tooth with another one; yet, as we know so well, it is only a matter of time before that replacement manifests itself—ergo, we again suffer the pain and separation. We should agree, then, that seemingly, a tooth always remains an undeveloped part of us.

In my loneliness, when I came to the moment of truth, I found that I never developed as a heavy in the annals of crime—and was tired of the pains of separateness. I had my fling, and I got a bright shiny dime—figuratively speaking—for pay, and nine cents worth of kicks. I would always have been in the latent stage should I have continued in that path—the trail of guilt and greed and unmitigated evil—a path which in my inmost reflections, I never did really like. If by some fantasy through chimeras that shiny dime had turned into dollars and on into millions, and if I owned all the stolen automobiles, dope and strumpets in the world, I could never have self-respect if the gains and pleasures had arrived by way of nebulous sources. I could never manifest myself, the simple me, through criminal activity.

Word of the event—little Johnny's trip to the dentist—set off a chemical chain of soul searching thoughts that flooded the dark dungeon inside me where the seeds of repugnant things bred, and drowned that separateness. The insatiable desire to rebel against the mores of my community had been the primordial suppressor of the good in me—as there's always good where there's bad—and the unshackling of the good became a germane demand. "When I thought my soul was lost, my dungeon shook, and my chains fell off," James Baldwin said in The Fire Next Time. This describes my present feelings; I have love and respect for everyone, and the proper mixture for the restorative solution was as simple as pulling a milk-tooth.

. . . . finis

(Reprinted from *Marion Messenger*, Vol. II, No. 3, August, 1964, United States Penitentiary, Marion, Illinois.)

Flop House

Tom Redgate

A FLOP HOUSE is a place where you meet a stone-faced, cold-eyed proprietor. Clutching the price of your bed in your dirty and trembling hand as tightly as if Ma had sent you on an errand to the corner.

A flop house is a place that stinks of dirty bodies and decaying minds. And quite possibly of lost souls.

A flop house is a place that you slink out of during the day and crawl into in the night.

A flop house is a place that when you wake up in the morning you find that the guy aside of you has completely given up and has willed himself to die during the long night.

A flop house is a place where everybody sleeps with their shoes tied to some part of their anatomy, just to insure the fact that they will be there in the morning.

A flop house is a place that you sleep in your own vomit, and worse.

A flop house is a place where nobody ever removes their clothes.

A flop house is a place where addled brain winos sit around and compare wine sores.

A flop house is a place that you wake up in at 3 AM, in your own private gethsemane, with your every nerve screaming and twitching for just one, Oh, please God, drink.

A flop house is a place where you slap angrily at a bedbug because the other animals that are irritating your body are too small to find.

A flop house is a place where the "wet-brain" shuffles back and forth in an alcoholic limbo.

A flop house is a place where you will sit on the edge of your bed, bowing and paying court to a sloppily drunk old man, simply because he will feed you an occasional drink.

A flop house is a place that sometimes the beds are so dirty and damp, that as filthy as you are, you would prefer to sleep on the floor.

A flop house is a place where the "jack-rollers" move stealthily through the night, cutting out your pants pockets for your pennies and nickles.

A flop house is the place where you throw a rum fit.

A flop house is the place where all of the crawling and slimy things come at night and creep into your eyes, ears, nose and mouth, while you screamingly try and fight them off.

A flop house is a place where the good morning cry is "I've got eight cents towards a jug!"

A flop house is the most horrible and loneliest place in the world.

So help me.

(Reprinted from *Weekly Progress,* Vol. 45, No. 3, January 17, 1964, Southern Michigan Prison.)

"THIS SHOOTS THAT 'MAN CANNOT LIVE BY BREAD ALONE' THEORY ALL TO BLAZES."

D. Fletcher, *MP News* (Montana State Prison; November, 1963), p. 20.

Time Is a River

KEN WESLEY

Time is a river.

Welling forth from the Springs of Innocence, it flows implacably, infinitely, along its predetermined course to disappear into the Sea of Destiny.

We, frail, infinitesimal motes of dust, conceived at the Springs, ride the crashing, bobbing waves, traveling on the ever-flowing River of Time, phantom voyagers creating not a single ripple in the tumultuous pounding surface.

Time, the river, is a ruthless master of all. From the infinite springs of its inception to the infinite vortex where it endlessly whirls, it spews forth other currents that merge, blend and become composite parts of the whole of the infinite stream from which they spring, rolling, tossing, forever flowing.

In our callow youth we naively attempt a hastening, urgently spurring the stream to greater speed, spurning the turbulent, frothing waters of adolescence, grasping for the tranquility of adulthood. We put our puny strength, impatient in our journey; faster, faster, even faster, we cry.

Time is a river.

It flows at a predetermined speed, heeding not the exhortations of the surface voyagers. It accepts our passage, charts our course, and heeds us not.

Slowly, inexorably, the river winds, and we travel farther and farther from the Springs of Innocence. We pass through the Inlet of Awareness, hardly noticing the passing, and arrive at the Streams of Decision. Here the voyager has the choice. The River of Time splits into many diverse streams, all having different courses, but all traveling at the same rate of speed.

No matter which stream we take, we eventually arrive at the Lake of Adulthood. Here we tarry, blissfully ignoring the river. The current seems abated, we feel marooned. Still the river moves, neither slackening nor quickening. And, in spite of our self-induced delusions we still move with it.

We arrive at the Lake of Adulthood by many different routes, all connected with main stream—the River of Time. Some routes take us past the Shoals of Despair, or the Reefs of Antipathy, making our journey seem long and tiresome. Other routes run blithely along through the Valley of Serenity or bubble past the Fountain of Happiness, making our trek into the Lake of Adulthood pleasant and all too swift. No matter which route brings us to our destination in the Lake of Adulthood, we soon pass on.

We no longer urge speed, we no longer exhort the River of Time. But, still it moves, at the same predetermined speed, on the same foreordained course. We try to ignore it, but we cannot. We are still voyagers on its ever-moving surface. As it moves, we too must move. It twists and turns, moving. We too are moving—moving slowly away from the placid Lake of Adulthood.

The river seems to quicken. It is approaching the swirling foaming rapids—the Rapids of Old Age. We try to hold it back, fearful and afraid. We protest that the river is moving too fast, much, much too fast. We turn, in a vain attempt to fight the current, striving to return to the serenity of the Lake of Adulthood, or better yet, to the Springs of Innocence. We cry, we wail and scream in frustration, for there is no return. We are shackled to the river, slaves to its moving currents. The River of Time flows in only one direction.

We pass quickly, too quickly, through the Rapids of Old Age. We fight the passage with all our strength, but in vain. We are infinitesimal and our strength is to no avail. We are buffeted and pounded, twirled and tossed, and finally brought to rest in the calm waters of the Lagoon of Dreams—destiny is at hand. Then slowly, or swiftly, as the case may be, we pass over the Falls of Peace and land at last in the swirling waters of the Sea of Destiny, completing our journey on the River of Time.

Time is a river.

It springs eternally from the Springs of Innocence, disappears eternally into the Sea of Destiny. It is an imperturbable, relentless current, unhampered in its flow by the millions of microscopic voyagers traveling with its flow.

(Reprinted from *Courier*, Vol. VII, No. 6, Fall, 1964, Maryland Penitentiary.)

Sister of the Brave

S. J. Gonzales

THE BEST PLACE is the old railroad station," Joseph George said. "Nobody goes near there anymore."

"All right," Jimmy Malone agreed; "I've got a new safety razor blade."

"Well, O.K.," Joseph George said disdainfully, "but a hunting knife is better. That's what the Indians use."

"Couldn't find it. I haven't found out where my dad keeps it."

"Well, let's go," said Joseph George, "before Patricia sees us."

They bobbed and weaved along the narrow trail through the tall weeds near the Union Pacific Railroad tracks that twisted through Cayuse, Oregon, on the Umatilla Indian Reservation. It was a July afternoon, hot and sweaty, with an occasional gust of wind from the north.

During the war years the little railroad station had been open for business and an east bound and a west bound train stopped daily; but now the little station was abandoned and each train roared through Cayuse with a clicking and a clacking of steel wheels upon steel rails.

"See anyone near the crossing?" asked Joseph, peering through the weeds at the path along the railroad tracks.

"No," Jimmy answered; "but we'd better hurry because old Sam Moses comes along here every day."

"Sam Moses and my dad are blood brothers. He wouldn't tell anybody."

"Well, if we're going to be blood brothers let's get it over with," Jimmy Malone urged. "If my dad found out I've been near the tracks, he'd tan me."

A snapping popped in the weeds and both boys spun around and listened.

"What was that?" Jimmy Malone whispered.

"Aw, some cat chasing a rat."

They came out of the weeds on the west side of the abandoned station, crouched and ran to the window, the panes of which had long been broken by the vibration from Diesel engines, clanking freight cars, and Indian youths improving their rocksmanship. The window was low and entry into the deserted station presented no difficulty.

Both boys were fifteen years old and both were natives of Cayuse, Oregon. Joseph George was a member of the Nez Perce Indian Tribe of Idaho that had amalgamated with the Walla Walla and the Umatilla Tribes of Washington and Oregon. Jimmy Malone was a member of the O'Hallahan Tribe of County Cork Ireland that had amalgamated with the Malone Tribe of the United States. Joseph George's father owned one-hundred acres of non-deeded farm land and Jimmy Malone's father rented the one hundred acres and hired people to grow wheat on it.

"I hope Patricia didn't see us leave Minnie Whitebull's house," Jimmy said, and crept over to a dusty table near the center of the old depot. "She always follows me."

"I'm glad I don't have any kid sister," Joseph said. "I wouldn't have any fun if she followed me everywhere I went."

Jimmy Malone unwrapped a safety razor blade and the boys eyed each other several moments in silence. Then Joseph George unbuttoned his shirt sleeve and bared his right wrist. The distant wail of a Diesel engine sounded outside the window.

"Let's get it over with," Jimmy Malone said with a sigh. "The quicker, the better."

"O.K.," agreed Joseph as he reached for the razor blade. "This will make us blood brothers for all times; not for just a little while."

"I know," Jimmy retorted. "Let's get it over with."

Joseph George held his right hand palm up and cut a small cross on his wrist, then gave the razor blade to Jimmy Malone who in turn cut a small cross on his right wrist. Then they held their wrists together, first the one on the other and then the other on the one, symbolic of two bloods becoming one blood.

"I just thought of something," Joseph George said; "I just thought about the test of bravery."

"Oh, that's the way the Indians did in the old times before we were born," Jimmy said. "There're no enemy tribes to fight now."

"I know. But my dad and his blood brothers found a way to test their bravery, and we . . ."

"I saw what you did with that safety razor," came from a babyish voice at the window.

The blood brothers stared in surprise!

"Patricia," Jimmy said, "didn't Daddy tell you to stay away from the railroad tracks?"

"Yes, and he told you too," she smiled. She was seven years old, red headed, and dominated everyone on the reservation.

"But I'm older," Jimmy reminded her; "I know better than to go upon the tracks."

The boys stepped out of the window onto the ground, and Jimmy grasped Patricia's right hand and led her toward the trail in the tall weeds.

"Now go back to Minnie Whitebull's house and wait for us," Jimmy said softly and released her hand. "When we come back, I'll buy you ice cream."

"I don't want to go back. I want to stay with you," she smiled; "and I don't want ice cream."

"Daddy and Mom told you to do what I tell you to do. Now go back to Minnie's house and wait."

"I won't," she answered.

Joseph George turned to Jimmy Malone with a wide smile, and knelt before the little girl. "I want you to do me a big favor, a favor I wouldn't ask anyone else to do for me."

Patricia looked into his brown face, but made no reply.

"Take this quarter and go to O'Neil's store and buy five packages of chewing gum and take them to Maggie Shippentower."

The little girl closed her tight hand into a fist over the quarter.

"Remember, I wouldn't trust anyone else to do this for me," said Joseph George. "But I trust you because you are my friend, aren't you?"

"Yes," Patricia said, her voice just above a whisper.

"All right. Now hurry up because Maggie is waiting for the chewing gum."

Patricia walked to the trail and the boys watched her until she was no longer visible in the tall weeds. The wail of a Diesel engine came from Mission, five miles west of Cayuse.

"I've got to hand it to you, Chief," Jimmy Malone said; "That was a good trick you played on Patricia to get rid of her."

"No trick," Joseph George said. "Indians learn about squaws early. Always make them feel important and they'll do anything you tell them."

The Diesel blasted two longs, a short, and another long wail as it came out of the curves between Mission and Minthorn Junction.

The boys neared the tracks and saw the tiny blur of the Portland Rose, the fastest train from Portland, Oregon, to Cheyenne, Wyoming.

"There it comes!" shouted Joseph George. "There comes our bravery test!"

"What're you talking about?" his blood brother asked, a note of perplexity in his voice.

"Let's stand in the middle of the track and see who chickens out before the train gets to that fourth telegraph pole."

Jimmy Malone noticed the size of the train increasing in the distance. "What happens if we leave the track before the train reaches the fourth pole?" he asked.

"We're chicken," Joseph George said harshly. "We're cowards."

They stepped over the rail into the middle of the railroad track, folded their arms across their chests, and faced the oncoming Diesel engine passenger train. The tall weeds bowed and swayed under a gust of wind, and a crow perched atop the old railroad station cawed an alarm.

The train was now in the three mile straight stretch of track and the Diesel engines roared in a heavy drone. As it reached the eleventh telegraph pole, ninth pole, eighth pole, seventh pole, sixth pole, fifth pole, fourth pole and they jumped from the track, turned and gasped in horror . . .

One telegraph pole behind them, in the middle of the track stood Patricia facing the train, her arms folded across her breast.

Jimmy attempted to run to her but his legs refused to carry him. Joseph George opened his mouth to shout something but no sounds came out.

The train streaked past the third pole toward the little girl. The boys stood in panic, shocked at the sight before them. As it reached the second pole, the train wailed like some savage, frightened thing in the jungle. Then, with utmost calm and reservation, Patricia stepped from the railroad track and walked toward the blood brothers.

The Diesel engine and coaches flashed past them in a drone and a clacking of steel upon steel, and then became small in the distance.

"I lost the quarter, Chief," Patricia said to Joseph George, "and when I came back for another one, you and Jimmy were standing and looking at the train. And I . . . I wanted to look at it too."

"Let's go home," Joseph George mumbled in a puny sigh.

The blood brothers walked limply from the track and into the tall weeds. They moved as if they had just released a burden they had carried a great distance. The joyous cries of playing children and the short barks of a dog came to meet them and to welcome them from where they had no desire of returning.

"Don't tell Daddy I was near the railroad, Jimmy," Patricia said just above a whisper. "I'm scared. I'm scared he'll spank me."

(Reprinted from the Joliet-Stateville *Time*, Vol. 6, No. 9, September, 1964, Illinois State Penitentiary.)

Her Lawn Canopy

D. C. JENSEN

THE OLD MAN sat on a pickle barrel in the damp, dim cellar of his sister-in-law's house. She has no right to talk to me like that, he thought as he stared into the gloom around him. Just who does she think she is, anyway? She may own this house but she is my brother's wife, and it was he who asked me to come and stay here for awhile until I get back on my feet again.

That woman gives me a pain in the ass! God, is she sick! Always hinting that my brother is so much better than I am . . . Oh, she never comes right out and says it but I know she thinks it.

Is it my fault that he married her and took over the business that her father left her? I might have married her (God forbid!) if he hadn't have come along first. Anybody could have, for that matter.

Oh, I know her kind. A warm bed can be awfully cold when you're in it alone. And now she's been married to him for 27 years, and since she's getting bored she packs all the boredom into a neat little bundle and ever-so-often presents it to me in the form of a tirade—a verbal enema to cleanse and purify her system.

But this morning she went too far! All I did was spill an ashtray on the carpet in the living room. I don't even mind the screaming so much, but when she called me a "dirty old bum!" that was too much . . . That's it!

What does she mean, OLD? Doesn't she remember that I am only three years older than she. She ought to know how it feels . . . Why, god, if I ever called her OLD, I'd be here in this cellar for the rest of my life.

Well, the hell with her! I'm just going to stay down here. This time she's gone too far . . . OLD! Huh? . . .

A fly began to buzz around the old man's head. It flew in lazy circles, sometimes coming near, sometimes arcing out for a full swing, diving and climbing as it went on its way.

"Well, well," said the man out loud, addressing the fly, "Isn't it kind of late in the year for you to still be flying around? I thought all you guys just naturally hung it up after summer is gone."

144

The fly made a large, slow circle, disappearing into the darkness of the cellar for a bit, and then reappearing in front of the old man. "Yeah," he sighed, "you're flying pretty slow, there. I guess you're getting old yourself."

The fly hovered in front of the old man, making several small, lethargic circles before his eyes.

"You're lucky, though, fly," the old man smiled. "At least you don't have a she-fly to get on your nerves all the time . . . Boy, fly, are you ever lucky!"

Over a window-sill in the corner of the cellar a spider was putting the final touches on an intricate web. Up and down, over and across, the spider spun until the web was finished. It was a masterwork of well-structured fibers, each mesh mathematically perfect and in its deadly place.

The old man looked up toward the window and as he saw the evil project being completed, a frown crossed his face. He held his breath for a moment, and then his eyes raced around the cellar searching for the single fly. He found the fly just in time to watch it begin one last, long, circle that ended abruptly in the middle of the spider web.

"Look out!" cried the old man, jumping up. It was too late . . . it was all over in a brief moment.

The old man looked around sheepishly, a little embarrassed at his own solitary outburst. He stood for awhile wiping his forehead. Then, dropping his hand to his side, he walked slowly to the stairs leading out of the cellar.

"Well," he muttered to himself. "I guess I had better get on upstairs and see what the old girl is up to."

(Reprinted from the *Terrescope*, Vol. V, No. 22, October 9, 1964, United States Penitentiary, Terre Haute, Indiana.)

A Lifer Speaks: "'Tis Christmas"

Jack Leighton

Tis Christmas,

And into this bastille flows a particle of the spirit the free world abounds in each Yule. The flurrying snow is seen dancing beyond the barred windows. Carols and greetings fill the airways and find their way into each cell. All touching and real however hard one's heart . . . .

Anticipation reaches a warm hum, as some hope for a gift, a visit, or a card from someone out of the past, if only to say they remembered . . . And even the toughest con was seen bartering for better cards and deeper verses to send to a loved one . . . , a child . . . , a friend.

And while children and joyous adults the world over peer for a glimpse of a santa or wrap tenderly a gift, so too does the convict feel Christmas . . . For he dreams, and his most cherished memories become vivid . . . , almost a touchable reality . . . , a hand to hold by the fireplace, a face to see happy, an embrace that means forever.

The time of year to avert and forget is here, for it is the time of loneliness and love . . . , fear and need . . . , fantasy and reality . . . , doubt and hope. We turn our backs to Christmas, then peer over our shoulders . . . We close our eyes, but listen for its sounds . . . We darken our cells and pray a hand will place a postal message on our door, from someone we know . . . , someone we remember, someone we love . . . Someone, we hope, remembers and tries to love us, even in prison, for each of us is just a man, who is moved by the little things of every day, when once a year "Tis Christmas."

(Reprinted from the *Bridge*, Vol. 4, No. 4, December, 1964, Connecticut State Prison.)

Spur of the Moment

How many times have I . . .

. . . settled back and watched the smoke, from countless cigarettes, rise into the overhead cell-light, disappear, and sent myself with it . . .

. . . ridiculed God; to be one of the guys; and then prayed, when lights were out, for forgiveness and understanding . . .

. . . rolled cigarettes and almost blew my top when the glue on the paper didn't hold . . .

. . . thought of revenge to one and all; then realized that I was here because of my own fallacies . . .

. . . wanted to listen to a program of my own choosing on the radio . . .

. . . screamed silently for release . . .

. . . wondered what movie was on the late show . . .

. . . wanted a cold beer while I was reading or just taking it easy along about eight in the evening . . .

. . . started to write a letter, realized there was nothing to write about, and gave up until the next time . . .

. . . thought of the ones that I love and have loved and what they were doing at the same moment that I was thinking of them . . .

. . . wanted a deck of cards . . .

. . . thought (and prayed) that today a miracle would happen and they would grant me an early parole . . .

. . . damned them because I had to shave in cold water . . .

. . . planned my future and then only do it again the next night with entirely new concepts . . .

. . . told myself that the only way that I would return here was on a slab . . .

. . . for the want of my woman, indulged in hours of self-pity . . .

. . . counted the years, months, weeks, days, hours, minutes and seconds until I would be free again . . .

. . . said that I was going straight when I got out . . .

. . . wanted a cup of hot coffee when I arose in the morning . . .

. . . wondered what sort of changes would occur in my mental outlook, if any, due to my time spent in prison; would it change those on the outside in their former feelings towards me; or mine for them? . . .

. . . planned what I would do on the first day that I am out of here . . .

. . . said silently, yet longed to be heard, to those I have hurt, to please forgive me . . .

(Reprinted from the *Courier*, Vol. VII, No. 4, Spring, 1964, Maryland Penitentiary.)

"Okay, Kingston, get off the wall and out of that costume––the Christmas play was last week!"

Bob Matlock, The *Forum* (Nebraska Penal Complex; Christmas, 1964), p. 10

Jungle

(Author Unknown)

Taken
From my home
Imposed
Into one
Not my own
Suffering
Abusements
All kinds
From the hands
Of educated minds
In this jungle
Of intellect
Egos breed atrocities
And the atrocities
In turn . . .

(Reprinted from the *Insider*, Vol. XXV, No. 8, September, 1964, D. C. Jail.)

A Summer Dream

S. A. GERACE

It is summer
And as I write, I feel
The warmth and tenderness of the playful breeze
The hidden love of the smiling sun
The ecstacy of the song that
Escapes the birds and drifts in my window
The tiny bugs, they scuttle itinerantly
Cool and happy as snowmen
Dressed like lollipops in red,
Green and yellow wrappers
Soaking in the world of love like a sponge

I lie here
My tiny bunk in a tiny cell
And write impromptu words
Words that are not said but felt
Oh hurry time!
A man is alive today and dead tomorrow
Today is so damned short, tomorrow is forever
I want to speak—thoughts, long bottled up
Come tumbling out of my mouth like acrobats
To disappear like footsteps on a beach
My words dart out and
Fly around the cell like helpless creatures
Oh hurry time!
Let me free for life is running
Running, Running, Always running!

(Reprinted from the Joliet-Stateville *Time*, Vol. 6, No. 10, October, 1964, Illinois State Penitentiary.)

Walls

J. Clausell

Let not your eyes rest upon these walls
Behind which you have concealed your shame
The shame of lies and injustice, hypocrisy
That glibly you would deny; but behold!
The sky shall bear witness, and be not daunted
Nor shall the sun refuse to luminate, the cold
Cruel darkness that lurks in the social soul.
Why? Shall you wonder in your whims—
Who—what soulless things have we interred there?

  The earth is not forgetful
She shall ever remember, those who are her own.
The human body is not soulless, though some
Have fallen in the race, are beaten and bested.
You have disinherited them entombed here
Those whom your world no longer mourns
Demurely attired in the black virtue of her
Glorious widow's weeds.

  This is the hell of Dante's inspiration.
Steel shall be a sacred symbol, of this generation.
But walls, how high, shall not hold back corruption.
The human mind is the monstrosity, it creates
All forms that time and eternity shall wear.
I have learned to live here, and I know
The filthy flow of empty days, how they merge
And sink down into the stench of limbo; I, then
Shall be your convict, and you my Nemesis,
But let us remain quiet, let us not question,
Lest in the fearful silence of our beating heart
Each perceives the other's guilt, and lose
Against our mounting wager.

I do not cry. For tears
Are only dry puffs of dust, rendering our visages
A pale and ghastly green, a nameless ugliness.
Hold, then, the sigh within the throat, though
It makes the words harsh and hoarse with no gentleness
And the prayer shall be too heavy to rise on high
But down into the bowels of earth let the iron balls form.

Stand behind me. I shall not look back.
Let the crepe curtain be drawn, and the years of history
Be dead years, stretching austerely, across massive
Frozen meadows; and let nothing be held dear:
Not youth, nor the singing landscape, and placid streams.
Let each shrinking vista, vanish, where manhood died,
Crushed in mortal anguish.

Flagellate me with your taunts and scorn
But still your walls are not high enough, to ostracize
That monster most fearful to your heart. Yes,
How true: my bones shall become brittle with age
And my mind a feeble and impotent thing, and to death
At last I shall succumb; but the wolves within you
Shall not die. What, then, shall you answer
To my query? Can maleness be inverted? Or
Shall the city of Sodom be resurrected?

Shrieks and screams I have heard
Rending my nights asunder, and by my door
I have crouched into the wee hours, wondering:
The child in man is dead, and now, only
In man a howling carcass lives: Fate has etched
Upon this solid figure, brutal lines and deep
Knife wounds that fester, running supperation.
Justice rides my shoulder, and taunts me with
Her howling hideous laughter, and in her cortege

Brutal death wears a general's commission
With shotgun cocked and deadly aimed, at he
Who dares protest her vicious outrage:
            Recant! Recant! Recant!

(Reprinted from *Courier*, Vol. VII, No. 6, Fall, 1964, Maryland Penitentiary.)

"I think this is going to solve my smoking problem!"

Bob Matlock, The *Forum* (Nebraska Penal Complex; May 2, 1964), p. 2

Introspection

Nelson Crawford

I AM A PRISONER.

My mind is made captive by ridicule.
Ridicule that has caused me to erect bars inside my skull so my
thoughts cannot escape. Ridicule that has caused my mind to hiber-
nate like a fat, burly bear full of summer feedings, tossing and
turning in a winter sleep he cannot understand.
Ridicule that accepts the ridiculous and makes a
mockery of the mighty.
My body is made captive through the strength of
steel bars and stone walls. The greys and
greens of my prison bend my back with a weight I can hardly bear.
The bars before me, straight and slender and numerous as
young, green shoots in a field of wheat, are beautiful in their
somber. The walls of stone that surround me are majestic and
lonely in their starkness.
The confines of my cell are narrow and small.
I am alone.
The imprisonment of my mind is a far worse thing.
It is far worse because I have willingly sacrificed myself to the
vicious whirlpool of ridicule. Sacrificed and recoiled from sacrifice.
There is no beauty in this prison. There is no majesty.
There is only bleak ugliness and the fury of hate.
The bars are tangled, intertwined ribbons of hate.
Hate so furious it twists the features of my face like those of a mad-
man in his fits of insanity. My skull is the walls. Walls so dread
they furrow my brow like a newly plowed field awaiting the seed of
thought.
Walls that encompass my mind with a barrier so high
escape would seem impossible.
Yet, thoughts do escape.
They emerge from the blast furnace of my mind burnt and bent,
humpbacked and strong.
They come forth like a convict released from a life

sentence, sniffing the cool, clean air of freedom only to be bom-
barded by the ignorance of men who have never thought. They
emerge to proclaim my beliefs, my ideals, to people who just don't
care.
They come forth to offer the gift of myself, only to
suffer the wounds of laughter.
I am not willing to loose the bonds of hate that
bind them, yet they burst into freedom like a brook that tumbles
and leaps in flight from its prison on the mountain top. I am not
willing to release them, yet they erupt from my mind like the spew-
ings of a volcano as it asserts its mastery over the earth below.
I cannot contain them.
Therefore, I say Damn to ridicule!
Damn to prejudice! Damn to ignorance!
Damn to the smug self-satisfaction of conceit!
I will lower the bars of my hate. I will tear down the walls that close
off the sight of freedom. I will remove the shackles that cuff my
mind.
I will loose my thoughts
and my mind will rest.

(Reprinted from *New Era*, Vol. XVIII, Nos. 1–2, Summer, 1964, Leavenworth, Kansas.)

The Old Man—Elegy

Wayne R. Williams

The old man used to
Walk through the park—
On days when he was lonely—
(As old men often are)
    Where the sound of the boys and girls
At play—
    Would gladden his heart
He used to walk—
    with his cane, and his dog
    and his old felt hat
up and around
    Old East Rock Park—
He would walk along the stream
    (on days when it was warm)
and pause—
To watch the falls of Old Lake Whitney
there—
The old man used to
Walk through the park
On days when he was lonely—
(As old men often are)   But now—
He does not walk   And he's never, ever Lonely—

(Reprinted from the *Lens*, November, 1964, United States Penitentiary at Lewisburg, Pennsylvania.)

CHAPTER 6

Administration of the Penal Press

A very large segment of the population of every prison believes that the newspaper should operate as a bulwark for them against the administration. . . . This prevailing attitude causes many inmates to scorn the prison newspaper, and regard it with suspicion as a sort of administration "Trojan Horse" whose sub rosa *purpose is to convince them against their will that the Garden of Eden was a Bowery flophouse compared to dear old "Muckamuck Prison."*—Joe Lucas, "The Iron Voice," MP News, Montana State Prison, November, 1963

IN HIS COMMENTARY on the penal press, Joe Lucas went on to decry the fact that inmates just wanted the prison publication to be "a handy outlet for the everyday gripes and deep-seated resentments by giving the administration plain HELL. . . . The fact that the prison newspaper avoids attacking anyone is considered, by some, prime evidence that it is essentially pro-administration, and thus anti-inmate." Lucas, who said he was the "father of one prison magazine and the former editor of another" concluded that in actuality, "the prison newspaper

157

is pro-administration, but it is also pro-inmate, and must rigidly adhere to this policy in order to fulfill its primary function as a reliable information medium."

Editor Lucas' reflections, based on his experience in the prison editor's chair, brought him to a sound and logical conclusion. A prison publication must, indeed, be pro-inmate and pro-administration. Only then is it operating in the interest of the public that provides the institution with its support; it must speak as an institutional voice, advocating measures that further all elements of the institution. This eminently worthy conclusion is obviously rather easy to arrive at, but exceedingly difficult to administer to fruition. Problems associated with the administration of prison publications are numerous, but none is more complex or difficult than the control of content so that it is in the best interest of the inmate, the administration, and the public.

THE PROBLEM OF CENSORSHIP

Content control, whether it be called censorship, advice, direction, persuasion, or supervision, is an almost universally accepted practice of prison administrators. The attitudes of prison officials vary widely with regard to the method or degree of this control, but on the whole there is agreement that it is their responsibility to exercise it.

In most instances, the responsibility for reviewing material before publication is delegated by the warden to an assistant, with that person having full censorship power. In some states, however, this pre-publication review extends all the way to the department of corrections in the state capital. Carried to this extreme, the censorship operation delays a staff to such a degree that production of a timely newspaper is almost impossible. And sometimes such censorship stems from the desire to "build a good image" for the persons involved, and not to protect the public's interest. But, on the whole, administrative control over penal publications has been exercised with restraint, good judgment, and commendable motivation. And, in at least one case, leadership from the state level has been responsible for introduction of the free-press principle into correctional institutions.

In February, 1966, pre-publication censorship of inmate publications was abolished for all correctional institutions in Indiana. At that time Indiana's new director of the Department of Correction, Bernard Dolnick, ordered the abolition of censorship of inmate publications in a program of change that also included elimination of mail censorship, corporal punishment, and solitary confinement. At the time of this writing, the no-censorship program has been under way for eight months without major incident.

Commissioner Dolnick, in response to queries about dangers of his censorship ban, said that he felt no real concern about the possibility of inmate publications creating unrest or threatening institutional security in any way. "Benefits of the new freedom far outweigh any potential threat to security," he said. He also pointed to a "built in" control that he said would deter editors from publishing dangerous material. "These men want their freedom, and they are not going to jeopardize early release possibilities by inciting a riot," he said. "And we always have our radio system to counter any problem that may arise. Freedom for the inmate publication and unlimited, uncensored correspondence are vital to a rehabilitation program, and society has to be prepared to take what slight risk might be involved. We can never teach our inmates responsibility without giving them some." [1]

It may be that in the not-too-distant future, along with further innovations in penology, censorship of penal publications will come to an end in other states. But whether there is formal censorship or not, the inmate publication's role in an institution (in fact, its very existence) will always depend upon the benevolence of an executive of the institution or the state's correction department. Controls may become indirect instead of direct. The large, bold "Censored" stamp may be replaced by unseen advice. Action against an editor may never be taken before publication; instead, only after irresponsible judgment has prevailed. But inevitably the inmate publication must function in the best interest of the institution and the public that supports the institution, or it will not be tolerated. Even the most liberal of prison administrators has a point beyond which he will not permit inmate publications to go. And the pressure from the inmate population that Editor Lucas decried tends to overwhelm the good judgment of some

1. Information presented here is from a telephone interview with Commissioner Dolnick, September 21, 1966.

convict editors. When it does, another penal publication becomes history.

How many penal publications have been suspended for going beyond reasonable bounds is impossible to determine, but there are several recent cases of record. For example, *Recount* of Colorado State Penitentiary, an excellent but rambunctious publication, was brought to an end in 1964 because of "some unfortunate misunderstanding between the editorial staff and the higher officials." Fortunately, it has now been replaced with the *Interpreter*, another excellent magazine. The *Hope Press* of Rhode Island was discontinued because, in the words of Deputy Warden Robert E. Houle, "Some of the 'hard core' wanted the paper to publish only articles which found fault with our parole . . . and other programs. Rather than continue with this monthly problem, we discontinued the paper." [2] As of mid-1966, the *Hope Press* was back in business. The Iowa *Hawkeye* was closed down in 1959 because of a derogatory article; it, too, was overhauled, reoriented, and reinstituted. At the Tennessee State Penitentiary, an otherwise excellent bi-monthly magazine, *Inside Story*, came to an end because of unacceptable content. It, too, has been replaced.

What makes content unacceptable? Where is the line that cannot be crossed without resulting in administrative action? Obviously answers to these questions differ among institutions, but the "inside story" of *Inside Story* is a good illustration of some commonly accepted boundary lines for most prison administrations. These lines are drawn at the point where personalities, especially outside public officials, are maligned, and at the point where a writer's criticism of the law, law enforcement, or prison administration would tend to encourage disorder or to increase the antagonism of readers toward specific authorities. A great deal of general criticism and general discussion of law enforcement and penology practices is often permitted, but specific local persons and situations cannot be singled out. In the case of the Tennessee publication, writers slipped beyond both these boundaries. [3]

2. Personal letter to the author, January 12, 1965.
3. Information about suspension of *Inside Story* is from a personal letter from Bill Dyer, public relations director for the Tennessee Department of Correction, dated September 29, 1965, and from undated photocopies of the articles from which quotations are taken.

In one instance, a writer first cited the population of Tennessee, then estimated that the 3,000 inmates of the state's penal institutions would have about 200,000 relatives and friends on the outside. "If these 200,000 people had a leader and would band together for the benefit of the inmates in these institutions," he wrote, "a prisoner would be highly respected and thought of as a human being. They could see to it that he got everything due him by law after he went to one of these institutions. The judge and jury saw to it that he got everything he had coming to him at his trial, and a little more in some cases."

He then went on to say:

> These people are paying the salaries of the governor, wardens, and guards of these institutions, as well as everybody else affiliated with them. But why is a prisoner not fed the same thing the guards and other officials eat? You people and my folks are footing this food bill, but their meals are much better than the inmates get. Do you want to see the guards eat better than me? After all, you are the ones paying for all of it.
>
> Our recreation has been cut down considerably for no reason at all, to my knowledge. Another thing, when a person is sentenced to prison he is told by the judge that if he keeps a clear record in prison he will be paroled when he becomes eligible for it, but this is not true. . . .
>
> Who is seeing to it that these things are being done? What are you doing about it? Nothing! I say get some leaders together and organize and see that these things are taken care of. . . .

Other writers criticized specific officials in this fashion (names of individuals and locales have been changed, but otherwise the items are verbatim):

> The sheriff of Blank County was arrested for transporting moonshine. Is it legal to arrest lawmen in that manner? I thought everything a lawman did was legal?

> Wilson Smith, Supt. of the Blank County Workhouse, was arrested a while back for driving while drunk. I wonder what will be done with Wilson. Will he be allowed to carry on his duties as Supt. if he gets 90 days?

Nashville, Tennessee, with 9, was tops in murders for the first three months of this year. I wonder if that number includes the ones beat to death at the jails and workhouses, or the ones committed by the police.

Aside from venting their spleens momentarily, the writers succeeded in doing nothing constructive for their peers or the institution, and they brought on the end of their magazine. Fortunately, in all the cases noted above, the discontinuations were followed, within a reasonably short time, by reinstatement of the publication or the substitution of another. And in each case, at least at the outset, the inmate staffs were directing their efforts toward constructive goals.

The prison official who is given the responsibility for supervision of the inmate periodical is in a difficult situation. He knows, of course, that he has the right to censor; if there is an essential element of prison confinement, it is the loss of ordinary liberty, including freedom of the press. But, on the other hand, he knows that a publication cannot be very effective internally if it is the "Trojan Horse" that Joe Lucas' readers were suspicious of. So he wants to permit maximum freedom of expression while assuring that the publication is constructive. And on an item-by-item basis, the evaluation is not easy. One item, while obviously not constructive, might not do any harm; and its inclusion might help win over the suspicious audience and avoid a long discussion with the inmate staff. But it could lead to another such item, then another, and soon all is lost. The official knows, too, that it is most difficult for an executive in charge of any organization to be reasonable about criticism; what might seem harmless may not seem so to the warden, superintendent, or director of the department of corrections. And he knows that, in spite of the fact that he has the right to censor, the American tradition is to dislike censorship and the censor, no matter what the situation.

Common situations that have brought out the censor's blue pencil are jokes that are too suggestive, negative comments about department of corrections programs, an overabundance of complaining, and a snide and cynical approach to institution problems.[4] In many instances

4. The Utah *Pointer News* had the joke problem in 1962; the Folsom *Observer* reported, "At times there are publication editors and/or staff writers who are extremely negative in their views toward CDC programs in general.

a considerable amount of time and effort is expended to avoid the outright act of censorship; at the federal institution at Lewisburg, Pennsylvania, for example, the chief problem cited was the "considerable staff time spent in encouraging positive thinking and reducing unwarranted expressions of injustice and resentment against authority." What is perhaps the best summary of the patient and thoughtful attitudes of many penal publication supervisors comes from the Chillicothe [Ohio] Federal Reformatory *Cross Roads*. The supervisor there, although he reported having disputes over content with his staff, said: "We have troubles from time to time, simply because occasionally the inmate's enthusiasm outruns his common sense. But these problems are not major. We simply ignore the article which raised the problem and spend a little time discussing policy with the individual." It is this basic tolerance, plus the willingness to take the necessary time to discuss policy with inmate staffs, that has made the penal press's history so long and fruitful.

OTHER SUPERVISORY PROBLEMS

Although censorship is listed as the most serious problem area for penal publication supervisors, other problems also exist in sufficient quantity to make life challenging. One editor of the *Eagle* at the Federal Reformatory for Women in Alderson, West Virginia, "got so involved in sports and other activities that she did not attend the staff meetings she herself called," and had to be replaced. A member of the Oklahoma *Eye Opener* staff was fired for improper use of the mailing privilege. The Nebraska *Forum* was called to task by a religious publication for the inmate movie selection as reported by the *Forum*. An instance of plagiarism embarrassed officials and staff of the Leaven-

---

This sometimes creates problems in that the publication reaches friends and relatives of inmates, is quoted from in the outside press, etc., and might be misconstrued as painting an actual picture of a situation or of having institutional administrative sanction."; Maryland *Soundings* had the problem of excessive complaining; and the Sierra (Cal.) *Nugget* told of "an instance where an editor made issue of problems in a snide and cynical way which did not aid in the satisfactory solution of the problems." These comments are representative of several whose problems were similar in nature.

worth *New Era*. And the day-to-day problems of financing, of getting suitable office space, and of getting the publication out on time are always at hand.

Considering the situation, it really is not unusual that the penal press causes some special administrative problems. Actually it is amazing that four out of five supervisors report that publications have *not* been a special administrative problem, and only one out of nine has had to replace a staff member or suspend the publication. In most cases, the successes have been possible because procedures have been set up that eliminate or lessen the problems before they occur. These include: the assignment of responsibility for publication supervision to a person skilled in human relations, the selection of editors who approach their work with reasonable attitudes, and provisions for the thorough understanding, *in advance,* of the limitations under which the publication must operate.

RESPONSIBILITY FOR SUPERVISION

There is no question that prison publications generally have found a home in the education department; slightly more than 78 per cent of them are administered by the supervisor of education, his assistant, or an instructor. Others who are assigned this responsibility include the associate warden in charge of treatment and the supervisor of vocational training, each of whom accounts for about 6 per cent of administrators. The remainder include the classification officer, administrative assistant to the warden, librarian, chaplain, recreation director, correctional specialist, camp counselors, outside journalists, and the warden.

Ultimate responsibility for all affairs of a prison rests with the warden, and many of them retain for themselves the right of final approval for certain types of publication material. Very few (about 5 per cent) want the opportunity to review all content, but some do ask their supervisors to bring to them for approval articles that are in any way questionable.

SELECTION OF THE EDITOR

A primary factor in determining the ease or difficulty of penal publication supervision—and in determining the value of any publications program—is the editor that has been chosen from the inmate population. He can, depending on his attitude, think he is constantly being censored and make life for the supervisor a steady series of debates over policy. If he is dilatory, he can be the source of constant concern about whether the publication will meet its publishing schedule. If he is not trustworthy, his special position can open the way for petty racketeering or other violations of institution regulations. If he is unskilled in his craft, he can produce a shoddy publication. But if, somehow, the prison rolls can yield a good editor who is directing his efforts constructively, then there is no serious conflict over censorship and no need for the blue pencil. He gets along well with the staff, and deadlines are met without prodding. He stays out of trouble and produces a publication that speaks well for the institution. The fact that so many supervisors were able to report that their publications create no special problems is an indication that staff selection procedures are generally sound.

In most cases, the publication supervisor—usually the head of the education program—has the leading voice in selecting the editor. He may have full authority, subject only to the warden's approval, or his choice may also need the blessing of the classification committee. The latter is usually the case if the editorship is a paid job; if it is a purely voluntary part-time activity, an academic instructor or the supervisor of education often has full jurisdiction.

There are some situations in which sole responsibility rests with the classification committee, or the warden, or an administrative group composed of the warden and his deputies. At the Utah Penitentiary, the editor is selected by the inmate council with approval of the warden. The editor then selects his own staff, again with the warden's approval. In other institutions, inmate participation is obtained by accepting recommendations of the outgoing editor. In virtually every case, the obvious necessity for the person supervising the publication to have primary authority in selecting the editor is recognized, although he may need the usually routine clearance of higher authority.

The criteria used in making selections go beyond the candidate's professional proficiency. Experience on the publication, writing ability, and a reasonable educational background are important, but most administrators are often as much, or more, concerned about other factors. "Behavior," "adjustment," "maturity," "responsibility," and "experience" were frequently listed as essentials and often in that order. Consequently, an editor ordinarily has been in the institution for some time before his appointment, in order for his behavior and adjustment record to be known. Experience on the publication as a voluntary contributor or subordinate staff member is usually the basis for evaluation of his maturity and willingness to accept responsibility. When the publication is a part of the education program, performance in class is also a helpful source of information. A strong desire on the part of the inmate to get the job is considered essential, but in a few instances lack of inmate interest has been a problem. Such cases have arisen in institutions where publications work is only a voluntary activity, and occasionally publications have been suspended when interest waned. With editorships classified as work jobs, the situation is usually reversed; the positions are eagerly sought. At the Ohio Penitentiary, for example, *OPNews* staff jobs are considered "promotions from any other job in the institution."

What kinds of men end up as prison editors? As one might expect, they have varied backgrounds. Prior to commitment, some were college students, one was a doctor of osteopathy, several were journalists or creative writers, one was an accountant, another was an auto mechanic, one had been a correctional officer at the state prison for fifteen years before his commitment to another institution for non-support. Their criminal backgrounds are equally varied. Although data here are limited (most institutions would not provide this information), there is an indication that those with serious offenses and long sentences predominate. In spite of the fact that this study included short-term institutions (and editors there would have to be short-termers), armed robbery and murder were the most frequently reported violations, and life and ten years were the most frequently reported sentences. The offenses of the 79 editors in state institutions about whom data were provided were:

Armed robbery	16
Murder	11 (6 first degree, 5 second)
Bad checks (ISF)	9
Illegal possession of dope	5
Forgery	4
Grand larceny	3
Assault and battery with intent to kill	2
Burglary	2
Embezzlement	2
Manslaughter	2

One conviction each for arson; aggravated assault; attempted manslaughter; attempted breaking and entering; auto theft; burglary (second degree); conspiracy; drunkenness; incest; larceny; unarmed robbery; petty theft; theft by deception; sex offence; sodomy; burglary and grand larceny; burglary and drug user; larceny and narcotics; kidnapping and shooting an officer; and forgery and robbery. In federal institutions, six were sentenced for auto theft, four for armed robbery, and one each for transporting stolen cars, transporting stolen property, counterfeiting, mail fraud, robbery and theft, and a fraudulent claim to the U. S. Treasury. The indeterminate nature of many sentences, with various minimums and maximums, makes detailed tabulation difficult, but, looking at minimums only, more than half the editors have sentences of five years or longer. It is also interesting to note that some editors are first offenders, some second, some third, and one was in prison for the fifth time.

Penal press supervisors agree that the criminal offense of an inmate is not a primary determinant of his capability as an editor. The inmate's institutional record is most important, with the other factors cited earlier also of value. There are conditions, however, that tend to make long-termers predominant in a list of editors. It takes time for an inmate to be able to demonstrate satisfactory behavior and adjustment and for him to build up some experience with the publication. And, except in juvenile institutions where editorships are often rotated so a maximum number may benefit from the experience, supervisors prefer an editor who can stay in the position for a reasonable length of time.

BASIC PUBLICATION POLICY

"All editors have been carefully selected, told of their responsibilities, and have been told of the importance of the paper. They have not let anyone down." This response to the query about what problems publications have caused came from the supervisor of the California *Conservation Conversation*. It illustrates the kind of response that all supervisors would like to be able to give. It also illustrates another important point of procedure.

Although editorial policy disputes may still arise, these can be kept to a minimum if editors are fully briefed, in advance, as to their responsibilities and the importance of their work. This briefing can take any form, but it is important that it be done before specific applications arise. It is also helpful if policy is in writing and available at all times. These written guidelines can be beneficial to all concerned: to the editor as he makes decisions about the usability of material and as he defends his selections to contributors and readers, and to the supervisor as he reviews the judgments of his editor.

One such set of guidelines has been in effect at the Massachusetts Correctional Institution at Norfolk since 1941. It is included here, not to show what specific publication policies an institution should have—these obviously must vary among institutions according to the character of the inmate population and other factors—but to indicate the scope of such statements: [5]

POLICY OF THE COLONY

For Guidance of the Editor and the Paper Committee
Upon its definition of News and the standards of the News-Values depend not only the character and tone of the paper, but

---

5. Undated letter from Benjamin Goldstein, Editor, the *Colony*, and Jerome J. Coughlin, Community Service Director, Massachusetts Correctional Institution, Norfolk.

whatever influence it may exert on the ideals and ideas of its readers.

It is believed that "The Colony" should handle but four types of material:

a) Institutional News—News of the Council and other inmate activities.

b) Constructive stories—Which should encourage men to do good when they are released.

c) Outside news of particular interest to inmates—Which would include excerpts of interpretations of new laws affecting prisons or prisoners.

d) Sports news—(General and Institutional) after approval by the Superintendent.

It is believed that the men in here are intensely interested in finding out how to get on after they leave here, and a story cannot be made effectively constructive unless it contains vivid elements of interest to the average man outside these walls.

A List of Rules

1. Items which deal with personalities
   a) The paper should have no personal viewpoints.
2. Keep clear of outside politics and political personalities.
3. It is considered bad form, even by inference, to condemn, defame, malign, or "ride" the Department of Correction, the Institution, the State and/or Federal governments, and/or the officials thereof. Anything that has reference to the Department of Correction or any of its Officials or to the Institution itself, must be approved by the Community Service Director and/or the Superintendent.
4. Create as much interest as possible in news of wholesome recreation, amusement, and avocational work, in order to aid inmate readers in solving the difficult problems of how best to use their leisure time. Outside news should ordinarily take second place.
5. Do not fake any story.
6. Do not take rumors for facts; verify them before printing.
7. Write sports stories so that they will be intelligible to the average reader and not merely to the fans.
8. If using a story from another publication, be sure to give

proper credit to the author and the magazine or paper in which
the story appeared.

9. All copy must receive the approval of the Community Service
Director.

—Approved by the Inmate Council, 1941

The most common source of difficulty with penal publications—
disputes over policy—are minimized if reasonable policies are established and made known in advance of application, if editors are
carefully selected, and if competent supervision is provided.

FINANCING AND FACILITIES

The American press has two traditional sources of revenue: advertising and circulation. Ordinarily the sale of space to advertisers is the
primary source, circulation a secondary one. With regard to both these
sources, the penal press has troubles. Certainly Pan American, Grey-
hound, Miami Beach hotels, and Cadillac are not going to invest in
penal press space; convicts may dream of travel, but they are not
immediate prospects. Virtually no advertiser, for that matter, would be
interested in a market of eight-cents-an-hour men, especially when any
purchases are made from a commissary where choice is limited. Even
the cigarette hucksters would find that the number of "roll your
own'ers" and users of "State Tobacco" reduces their potential sales to
a dismally low point. Thus, the possibilities for advertising revenue are
extremely limited; so limited that most penal publications make no
effort to obtain it. One publication that does, the Southern Michigan
Spectator, has sold space to such firms as a soft drink bottler, a writers'
magazine, a leathercraft kit-maker, a plastics corporation offering dis-
tributorships, and an aeronautics manufacturer for a public service
announcement. Even so, the *Spectator's* annual revenue from advertising and circulation *combined* was less than one-fourth of its budget.[6]

More effort is expended to get circulation revenue, but the majority
(81 per cent) do not bother with subscriptions either. Of those that do,

6. "Spectator Figures Noted," Southern Michigan *Spectator,* January 14,
1966, p. 1.

more than half charge only a token $1.00 per year. Funding of the prison press, therefore, is quite different from the outside press.

The primary revenue sources of the penal press are the "inmate benefit fund" and legislative appropriations. Although it goes under many names, most penal institutions have an inmate fund that is accumulated from commissary sales, craft shop sales, inmate entertainment productions, and similar sources. This fund is used to provide inmates with benefits approved by the administration and not usually available through appropriations. In some institutions, such as the Maryland Penitentiary, the inmate publication has been supported entirely from the inmate fund, with contributions being accepted from outside readers. In others, including the federal institutions, the newspapers and magazines are financed by a specific allotment from the institution's appropriated funds. In the federal institutions, the education supervisor provides the funds from his budget. In others, such as the Ohio Penitentiary, the funds actually come from both sources, as well as subscriptions. Here, costs are first met from appropriated funds. Then the deficit, after subscription income is figured, is prorated among inmate and outside readers and the portion chargeable to the inmates is transferred from the inmate fund.

In the state institutions, there seems to be a pronounced reluctance to consider inmate publications a legitimate recipient of tax monies, whereas there is no such reluctance among federal institutions. Until the view is accepted that periodicals published "by and for inmates" benefit the public also—not just the inmates—the penal press cannot achieve its peak potential.

Penal publications can be produced on a shoestring, and a great many of them are. One of the new entries into the field in 1966 got going on a spirit duplicator donated by an office supply firm, and even many of the long-tenured publications are still showing that exemplary content can turn up in mimeographed publications as well as in the four-color, printed showpieces. As a matter of fact, the squeeze of limited funds has forced more penal publications to mimeographing than to any other reproduction process.[7]

7. Approximately 44 per cent are mimeographed; 26 per cent are letterpress printed; 19 per cent are offset; 10 per cent are spirit duplicated. With an annual printing budget of only $200, Miss Marguerite Givens, supervisor

But the fact that good content can appear in the cheaply produced publications does not necessarily mean that these production methods are desirable. Where the acceptability of a publication is in doubt or of special importance, the graphics of its presentation become especially significant. For the penal press, with a very definite incentive to influence its readers, there is an unusual need for the best visual appearance. A finely printed, attractive, professional looking penal publication will have a better chance of accomplishing its goals, inside and out of prison, than one hand-cranked from an ancient mimeo machine.

SOME THOUGHTS FOR THE FUTURE

Since the *Forlorn Hope* made its debut in 1800 as America's first prison newspaper, the penal press has established itself as a respectable and worthwhile segment of this country's press. For more than a century and a half it has struggled to determine its legitimate goals, its unavoidable limitations, and its worthwhile potential. It still is, in many respects, an unsettled area of the fourth estate, its course not fully charted. But an impressive record of service in a strange setting for the press—a society so different from the usual—makes its future direction almost certainly one of still greater value.

The record of the penal press, as verified by analysis of its content and by the opinions of all segments of its public—convicts, prison administrators, and outsiders who have taken an interest in it— justifies some conclusions, observations, predictions, and hopes for it.

1. Penal publications have been effective as an internal communications medium. They have provided a means for prison officials to get

---

of education at the Federal Reformatory for Women at Alderson, West Virginia, was able to produce a mimeographed quarterly that contained excellent copy. Budgets of the printed quarterlies and the weekly newspapers often were $5,000 and more. During fiscal year 1965, for example, the SMP *Spectator* cost $5,536.37. It earned $1,312.73 from advertising and subscriptions; the operating deficit of $4,398.62 was drawn from the General Benefit Fund.

announcements and other important information to the inmate population; they have been effective supporters of worthwhile activities of the population, including blood donations, charitable activities, sports and recreation programs; they have been morale boosters in a society where this is especially important; and they have become a recognized part of the rehabilitative goals of most correctional institutions. In this last role, the role of influencing inmate readers toward rehabilitation, lies one of the greatest hopes for future service.

2. Penal publications, in situations where they have been encouraged to do so, have been effective devices for reaching the outside public with information from what is virtually a forgotten part of society. Many convict editors believe this is the most important activity of the penal press. Given proper guidance, the penal press can be much stronger in this area.

3. Penal publications are equal or superior to any of the arts and crafts as an outlet for creativity. The thought process involved in self-expression through writing is or can be an added plus for writing, and one that is not involved in other outlets. Of still more importance, in the views of the editors themselves, is the self-discipline that editing a publication teaches. Administrators agreed that this teaching of responsibility was an important contribution of publication editing.

4. It is to be hoped that all prison administrators will eventually consider the penal press sufficiently worthwhile to merit the time and funds it needs. Although more than half of the extant correctional institutions have publications, there should be still more, and they should receive increased financial support.

5. Many publications programs, though effective, could be improved. An ideal program would provide an internal communications device, preferably a newspaper, published weekly or more often. Frequency of publication is important for success with the internal objectives of a prison publication. A quarterly magazine directed mainly outside the prison could provide the necessary literary outlet and external communication device. Enough funds to make both internal and external publications sufficiently attractive in appearance to gain the quick respect of their readers should be provided. Because inmates and outside public both benefit directly or indirectly from the publica-

tions, it would seem reasonable that funds should come from both sources.

6. Ordinarily at least one inmate should be assigned to the publication on a full-time basis. Full-time assignments avoid some routine problems in meeting deadlines, provide a worthwhile work classification, and give the publication the status it needs for maximum effectiveness.

7. Wherever possible, the help of a professional journalist should be solicited. This outside help could be used most effectively to design a professional looking periodical and to set up the journalistic procedures necessary to maintain it on that level. The volunteer help of journalism educators or practitioners from nearby areas could be sought.

8. A central clearing house for the Penal Press organization, giving it the unity it needs for making maximum use of the potential of individual publications, would be helpful. Some Penal Press material is worthy of inclusion in all prison publications. This clearing house might also serve as the outlet for information from the penal press to sociologists, social psychologists, and others (students and professionals). A wider distribution among such persons of the more valuable essays by prisoners on serious subjects could be an important contribution.

9. Maintenance of files, including the circulation of publications to historical societies and libraries for preservation, should not be overlooked.

10. Penal press editors should continue to accept the challenge of making their products worthwhile ventures; the record of the past is commendable, and still more service is possible if editors work to keep their publications constructively oriented. Supervision, collaboration, and guidance from prison administrators should be accepted and put to use; all publications, including those outside prison walls, have restrictions under which they must operate. Although the restrictions on the penal press may be more numerous and more direct, they do not bar the performance of service to inside and outside populations.

11. Prison administrators, as they guide inmate publications, should permit a reasonable freedom of operation so editors may have

the respect of their audience. Other support should be adequate also. The penal press, in its history, has been like a plant that has grown from a field of stones. No one planted it there, but still it grew. And with some food and water (finances and facilities) and some air to breathe (reasonable freedom), it can grow into something of greater value than it has been before. Its past record merits future support.

APPENDIX A
A Directory of Correctional Institution Publications, 1966

THIS LIST of United States correctional institution publications was compiled from questionnaires (see Appendix B) sent to wardens or superintendents of all institutions listed in the August, 1965, *Directory of State and Federal Correctional Institutions*, published by the American Correctional Association. Respondents to the questionnaires were later asked to check their listing and to provide information about any other publications not then on the list. The few publications from county and military institutions were added in this fashion.

INSTITUTION	PUBLICATION TITLE	DATE OF FOUNDING	TYPE	FREQUENCY OF PUBLICATION	CIRCULATION
Alabama					
Alabama Boys' Industrial School, 8950 Roebuck Blvd., Birmingham 6	The *Boys Banner* [1]	1905	tabloid newspaper	monthly	650
Draper Correctional Center, Elmore	The *Reporter*	Oct., 1961	8½ x 11 magazine	bi-monthly	600
Kilby Prison and Receiving & Classification Center, Route 3, Box 115, Montgomery 36110	*Kilby Sun* [1]	Oct., 1961	tabloid newspaper	weekly	1,000
Alaska					
Adult Conservation Camp, Box 746, Palmer	*Williwaw Journal*	1962	8½ x 11 magazine	monthly	250
Arizona					
Arizona State Industrial School for Boys, Ft. Grant	The *Young Citizen*	1928	tabloid newspaper	monthly	2,500

176

Institution	Publication Title	Date of Founding	Type	Frequency of Publication	Circulation
Arizona State Prison, P.O. Box 629, Florence	The *Vanguard*	—	8½ x 11 magazine	monthly	—
	El Saguaro	—	8½ x 11 newspaper	bi-weekly	—
Arkansas	None				
California Ben Lomond Youth Conservation Camp, 13575 Empire Grade, Santa Cruz 95056	*CBL News*	July, 1958	8½ x 11	weekly	98–113
California Conservation Center, Box 790, Susanville	*Mountaineer*	June, 1963	8½ x 11 magazine	monthly	1,875
California Correctional Institution, Box 1031, Tehachapi	*Hilltopper*	1955	8½ x 11 newspaper	monthly	700
California Institution for Men, Box 128, Chino 91710	*Pioneer News*	1942	tabloid newspaper	monthly	—
California Institution for Women, Rural Route No. 1, Frontera	*Clarion*	—	8½ x 11 magazine	monthly	1,300
California Medical Facility, Box 568, Vacaville 95688	*Vaca Valley Star*	1955	8½ x 11 magazine	monthly	1,000
California Mens Colony, Box 836, Los Padres	The *Communicator*	—	8½ x 10½ newspaper	weekly	—
California State Prison at San Quentin, San Quentin 94964	*San Quentin News* [2]	Dec., 1940	tabloid newspaper	bi-weekly	7,800

Institution	Publication Title	Date of Founding	Type	Frequency of Publication	Circulation
California State Prison at Folsom, Box No. W., Represa	The *Folsom Observer*	1947	9½ x 12½ newspaper	bi-weekly	2,200
California Training Facility, Box 686, Soledad 93960	*Soledad Star-News*	—	9 x 12 newspaper	bi-weekly	2,144
Deuel Vocational Institution, Box 400, Tracy	The *Crossroads*	1950	tabloid newspaper	monthly	2,000
Fred C. Nelles School for Boys, 1102 W. Whittier Blvd., Whittier 90602	*Washington Dollar*	—	8½ x 14	irregular	—
	Hoover Blab		8½ x 14	irregular	—
Fricot Ranch School for Boys, San Andreas 95249	*Eagle Eye*	1959	8½ x 11 magazine	bi-weekly	400
Paso Robles School for Boys, Paso Robles 93446	The *Pathfinder*	Jan., 1964	8½ x 11 newspaper	monthly	200
Preston School of Industry, Rural Route, Box 5, Ione 95640	*Prestonian* [3]	1962	pocket magazine	monthly	1,000
Sierra Conservation Center, Box 497, Jamestown	The *Nugget*	Sept., 1965	8½ x 11 newspaper	bi-weekly	2,000
Southern California Reception Center-Clinic, 13200 S. Bloomfield Ave., Norwalk 90650	The *Tiki*	Sept., 1964	8½ x 14	bi-monthly	100
Southern Conservation Center, Box 368, Chino	*Conservation Conversation*	1964	8½ x 11 newspaper	monthly	1,150

Institution	Publication Title	Date of Founding	Type	Frequency of Publication	Circulation
Colorado					
Colorado State Penitentiary, Box 1010, Canon City	The *Interpreter*	1966	8½ x 11 magazine	bi-monthly	2,200
Colorado State Reformatory, Box R, Buena Vista	*Buena Vista Review*	1958	8½ x 11 newspaper	monthly	900
Lookout Mountain School for Boys, Drawer 272, Golden	*Columbine News* [3]	1957	8½ x 11 magazine	monthly	400
Connecticut					
Connecticut School for Boys, Meriden 06453	*Hilltop Hubbub*	1915	8½ x 11 magazine	monthly	650
Connecticut State Prison, Box 100, Somers 06071	*Weekly Scene*	1957	8½ x 11 newspaper	weekly	1,167
	The *Bridge*	1915	6¼ x 9 magazine	quarterly	1,700
Connecticut State Prison, Osborn Div., Hazardville	The *New View*	1959	8½ x 11 newspaper	weekly	300
Long Lane School, Box 882, Middletown 06458	The *Tower*	1955	newspaper	monthly	180
Delaware					
Ferris School for Boys, Faulkland & Centre Roads, Wilmington 19805	The *Ferris Wheel*	Dec., 1959	8½ x 11 magazine	quarterly	300
District of Columbia					
District of Columbia Jail, 200 19th Street, S.E., Washington 20003	The *Insider*	June, 1947	7 x 8½ magazine	monthly	550
District of Columbia Reformatory, Lorton, Va. 22079	*Time & Tied*	1946	8½ x 11 magazine	monthly	1,200

Institution	Publication Title	Date of Founding	Type	Frequency of Publication	Circulation
District of Columbia Women's Reformatory, Occoquan, Va.	*Her Echo*	1961	8½ x 11 magazine	quarterly	200
District of Columbia Youth Center, Lorton, Va. 22079	*Telstar*	1961	8½ x 11 magazine	bi-monthly	300
Receiving Home for Children, 1000 Mt. Olivet Rd. N.E., Washington 20001	*Receiving Home Herald*	Aug., 1965	8½ x 11 newspaper	monthly	200
Florida Apalachee Correctional Institution, P.O. Box 127, Chattahoochee 32324	*Apalachee Diary*	1950	pocket magazine	quarterly	550
Avon Park Correctional Institution, P.O. Box 1177, Avon Park 33825	*Dopester*	1958	8½ x 11 magazine	bi-monthly	950
Division of Correction Road Prisons, 620 S. Meridian St., Tallahassee 32304	*Road Prison*	1958	8½ x 11 magazine	monthly	—
	Caryville Criterion	—	8½ × 11 magazine	monthly	—
Florida Correctional Institution, Lowell 32663	*Fla-Co-Lo*	1957	8½ x 11 magazine	quarterly	300
Florida School for Boys at Marianna, P.O. Box 590, Marianna 32446	*Yellow Jacket* [3]	—	tabloid	bi-monthly	3,600
Florida School for Boys at Okeechobee, P.O. Box 1207, Okeechobee 33472	*TeePee* [3]	Dec., 1960	tabloid	bi-weekly	4,000

Institution	Publication Title	Date of Founding	Type	Frequency of Publication	Circulation
Florida School for Girls at Forest Hill, P.O. Box 1359, Ocala	*Forest Hill News* [3]	1952	8½ x 11 newspaper	quarterly	350
Florida School for Girls at Ocala, P.O. Box 1359, Ocala	*Acorn* [3]	1958	8½ x 11 magazine	monthly	450
Florida State Prison, P.O. Box 221, Raiford 32083	*Raiford Record*	1939	8½ x 11 magazine	quarterly	2,000
Georgia Georgia Industrial Institute, Alto	The *Beacon*	1949	tabloid newspaper	monthly	1,000
Georgia State Prison, Reidsville	The *Spokesman*	1939	8½ x 11 magazine	quarterly	2,000
Youth Development Center, P.O. Box 788, Milledgeville 31061	The *Criterion*	Sept., 1964	tabloid newspaper	monthly	700
Hawaii Hawaii State Prison, 2109 Kamehameha Highway, Honolulu 96819	*Pahao Press*	1935	9 x 7 magazine	quarterly	1,100
	Pahao Nuhou	1951	8½ x 11	bi-weekly	300
Honolulu Jail, Halawa, Aiea, Oahu 96701	*Halawa Bulletin*	Oct., 1962	tabloid	weekly	75
Kulani Honor Camp, P.O. Box 1721, Hilo 96720	*Voice of Kulani*	1950	8½ x 11 newspaper-magazine	bi-monthly	150
Idaho Idaho State Penitentiary, Box 1719, Boise 83701	The *Clock*	1947	8½ x 11 magazine	monthly	800

Institution	Publication Title	Date of Founding	Type	Frequency of Publication	Circulation
Illinois					
Illinois State Penitentiary, Joliet-Stateville Branch, P.O. Box 1112, Joliet 60435	*Joliet-Stateville Time*	1935	8½ x 11 magazine	monthly	5,500
Illinois State Penitentiary, Menard Branch, P.O. Box 711, Menard 62259	The *Menard Time*	Feb., 1934	tabloid	monthly	7,500
Illinois State Penitentiary, Pontiac Branch, P.O. Box 99, Pontiac 61764	*Pontiac Flag News*	Feb., 1964	tabloid newspaper	monthly	2,600
Illinois State Reformatory for Women, Dwight 60420	The *Pathfinder*	1949	8½ x 11 magazine	quarterly	400
Illinois State Training School for Boys, P.O. Box 122, St. Charles	*Hour Glass*	—	9 x 12 newspaper	monthly	—
Indiana					
Indiana Boys' School, Rt. 1, Box 2, Plainfield	*Boys' School Herald*	1900	tabloid	monthly	1,000
Indiana Girls' School, 2596 Girls' School Road, Indianapolis 46224	*Teen Times*	1964	pocket magazine	monthly	300
Indiana Reformatory, Box 28, Pendleton	*Pendleton Reflector*	1896	tabloid	weekly	3,300
Indiana State Farm, Box 76, Greencastle	*Hill Top Crier*	1934	8½ x 7 magazine	bi-weekly	600

Institution	Publication Title	Date of Founding	Type	Frequency of Publication	Circulation
Indiana State Prison, Box 41, Michigan City	*Lake Shore Outlook*	1949	tabloid	bi-weekly	5,200
	Encourager	1953	8½ x 11	quarterly	4,000
Indiana Women's Prison, 401 N. Randolph St., Indianapolis 46201	*15 Acres*	—	booklet	semiannually	300
Iowa Iowa State Penitentiary, Box 316, Ft. Madison 52627	*Presidio*	March, 1934	8½ x 11 magazine	monthly	1,500
Iowa Training School for Boys, Lock Drawer C, Eldora 50627	The *Echo*	1904	6 x 9	monthly	1,350
Iowa Training School for Girls, Lock Box 64, Mitchellville 50169	*Tattler*	1950	8½ x 11 pamphlet	bi-monthly	300
The Men's Reformatory, Box B, Anamosa 52205	*Hawkeye*	July, 1898	8½ x 11 magazine	monthly	1,500
Kansas Boys' Industrial School, Topeka 66608	The *Chronicle*	1933	10 x 13 newspaper	monthly	1,800
Kansas State Industrial Farm for Women, Lansing	The *Lancer*	Oct., 1965	8½ x 11 magazine	monthly	150
Kansas State Industrial Reformatory, Box 569, 500 S. Reformatory Ave., Hutchinson	The *Harbinger*	1950	8½ x 11 magazine	bi-monthly	2,400

Institution	Publication Title	Date of Founding	Type	Frequency of Publication	Circulation
Kansas State Penitentiary, Box 2, Lansing	*Stretch*	June, 1957	8½ x 11 magazine	monthly	2,000
Kentucky Alben W. Barkley State Camp for Boys, Kentucky Dam Village, Gilbertsville 42044	*Life at Boys Camp*	Nov., 1962	8½ x 11 magazine	monthly	300
Kentucky Diagnostic and Reception Center, Westport Rd., Louisville 40222	*Center Special*	1962	8½ x 11 magazine	bi-weekly	300
Kentucky State Penitentiary, Eddyville	*Castle on the Cumberland*	—	8½ x 11 magazine	monthly	500
Kentucky State Reformatory, La Grange 40031	*Skytower News*	1940's	8½ x 11 magazine	bi-monthly	550
Kentucky Village, Spurr Rd., Lexington 40505	*Ky. Village Broadcaster* [3]	Jan., 1955	8½ x 14 newspaper	monthly	850
Louisiana Louisiana Correctional and Industrial School, P.O. Box 1056, De-Quincy	The *Rebel*	1958	8½ x 11 magazine	bi-weekly	300
Louisiana State Penitentiary, Angola	*Angolite*	1952	8½ x 14	weekly	—
State Industrial School for Colored Youth, P.O. Box 3527, Baton Rouge	*Campus Newsletter*	—	8½ x 11 magazine-tabloid	quarterly	—

INSTITUTION	PUBLICATION TITLE	DATE OF FOUNDING	TYPE	FREQUENCY OF PUBLICATION	CIRCULATION
Maine					
Maine State Prison, Box A, Thomaston 04861	*Tommy-Town News*	—	8½ x 14 newspaper	weekly	—
Stevens Training Center, Hallowell 04347	*Spotlight on Stevens*	1965	8½ x 11 magazine	bi-monthly	800
Maryland					
Maryland Correctional Institution, Rt. 3, Hagerstown	The *Trumpet*	1954	8½ x 11 magazine	bi-monthly	1,200
Maryland Correctional Institution for Women, Box 535, Jessup	*Soundings*	1950	8½ x 11 magazine	quarterly	205
Maryland House of Correction, Box 534, Jessup	The *Conqueror*	1962	8½ x 11 magazine	quarterly	2,200
Maryland Penitentiary, 954 Forrest St., Baltimore	*Courier*	1952	8½ x 11 magazine	quarterly	4,000
Massachusetts					
Berkshire County Jail & House of Correction, Pittsfield	*Bars & Stripes*	March, 1965	8½ x 11 magazine	bi-weekly	75
Bristol County Jail & House of Correction, New Bedford	*Bristol Crier*	1963	8½ x 11 magazine	bi-weekly	500
Hampden County Detention Center, 51 E. Mountain Rd., Westfield 01085	*Bi-weekly Announcer*	Sept., 1965	8½ x 11 newspaper	bi-weekly	30
Hampden County Jail & House of Correction, Springfield	The *New Yorker*	1963	8½ x 11 magazine	monthly	200

Institution	Publication Title	Date of Founding	Type	Frequency of Publication	Circulation
Hampshire County House of Corrections, 50 Union St., Northampton 01060	*Union House*	1966	8½ x 11 magazine	monthly	—
Lyman School for Boys, Box 122, Westborough 01581	*Lyman Hawk* [3]	1965	8½ x 11 newspaper	bi-monthly	300+
Massachusetts Correctional Institution, Box 366, Bridgewater	The *Beacon*	Dec., 1960	11 x 17 newspaper	monthly	3,500
Massachusetts Correctional Institution, Box 00, Concord	*Our Paper*	1885	9½ x 13	monthly	400
Massachusetts Correctional Institution, Box 99, Framingham	*Harmony News*	1945	8½ x 11 magazine	quarterly	350
Massachusetts Correctional Institution, Box 43, Norfolk	The *Colony*	1935	tabloid	bi-monthly	2,600
Massachusetts Correctional Institution, Walpole, Box 100, South Walpole	The *Mentor*	1898	13½ x 19 newspaper	monthly	6,000
Massachusetts Prison Camps, Box 207, South Carver 02566	The *Camper*	April, 1966	8½ x 12 newspaper	monthly	—
Michigan Boys Training School, Lewis Cass Bldg., Lansing 48913	The *Enterprise*	—	tabloid newspaper	monthly during school	300

INSTITUTION	PUBLICATION TITLE	DATE OF FOUNDING	TYPE	FREQUENCY OF PUBLICATION	CIRCULATION
Cassidy Lake Technical School, R.F.D. 1, Waterloo Rd., Chelsea 48118	*Cassidy Lake*	1955	tabloid newspaper	weekly	245
Corrections-Conservation Camps, 6000 Maute Rd, Rt. 3, Grass Lake 49204	The *Camp Fire* [3]	1953	8½ x 11 newspaper	quarterly	300
Detroit House of Correction, Plymouth	The *Voice*	1930's	8½ x 11 newspaper	weekly bi-weekly	500
State House of Correction & Branch Prison, Marquette 49855	*Northwoods Bulletin*	1963	8½ x 11 newspaper	quarterly	2,000
	Weekly Progress	1938	8½ x 11 newspaper	weekly	2,000
State Prison of Southern Michigan, 4000 Cooper St., Jackson 49201	The *Spectator*	1930	tabloid newspaper	weekly	9,000
Michigan Reformatory, Ionia 48846	*Hill Top News*	1928	9 x 12 magazine	monthly	2,500
Minnesota Home School for Girls, Sauk Centre	*Campus Happenings*		8½ x 11 magazine	bi-weekly	250
Minnesota Reception & Diagnostic Center, 7525 Fourth Ave., Circle Pines	*Lino Syndicate*	1963	8½ x 11	monthly	250
Minnesota State Prison, Box 55, Stillwater	*Prison Mirror*	1887	tabloid	bi-weekly	2,527
State Reformatory for Men, Box B, St. Cloud	The *Reformatory Pillar*		tabloid newspaper	bi-weekly	2,000

Institution	Publication Title	Date of Founding	Type	Frequency of Publication	Circulation
State Reformatory for Women, Box C, Shakopee	*Reflector*	1935	8½ x 11 magazine	quarterly	400
State Training School for Boys, Box 35, Red Wing	The *Riverside*	1894	tabloid	monthly	1,100
Thistledew Lake Forestry Camp, Box W10, Togo 55788	*Boondocker Times*	1961	tabloid newspaper	monthly	60
Willow River Forestry Camp, Willow River	*Informer*	1952	8½ x 11 newspaper	monthly	100
Youth Vocational Center, Route 4, Rochester	*Camburger* [3]	Aug., 1960	8½ x 14	monthly	150
Mississippi Mississippi State Penitentiary, Parchman 38738	*Inside World*	—	8½ x 11 magazine	monthly	—
Missouri Missouri State Penitentiary for Men, Box 900, Jefferson City 65102	*Jeff Town Journal*	—	tabloid newspaper	monthly	4,000
Moberly Medium Security Prison, Box 7, Moberly 65270	*Rocketeer*	Sept., 1963	11 x 15 newspaper	bi-weekly	750
Training School for Boys, Boonville	The *Campus News*	1950	21 x 28 newspaper	monthly	2,000
Training School for Girls, Chillicothe	*Campus Chatter*	Oct., 1965	8½ x 11 newspaper	monthly or bi-monthly	—
Montana Montana State Ind. School, Box 210, Miles City	*Boys' Messenger*	1889	8½ x 14	monthly	290

Institution	Publication Title	Date of Founding	Type	Frequency of Publication	Circulation
Montana State Prison, Box 7, Deer Lodge	*MP News*	Jan., 1962	pocket magazine	monthly	1,000
Montana State Vocational School for Girls, Rt. A, Box 30, Helena 59601	*Helena Valley Times*	—	8½ x 11 magazine	quarterly	—
Nebraska Boys' Training School, P.O. Box 192, Kearney 68847	The *Viking*	—	magazine	monthly	250
	The *Nebraskan*	—	annual, soft cover	annual	250
Girls' Training School, Geneva	*Ayweno*	—	8½ x 11 newspaper	irregular	—
Nebraska Penal and Correctional Complex, P.O. Box 111, Lincoln 68501	*Forum*	1938	tabloid newspaper	weekly	1,580
Nevada Nevada State Prison, Box 607, Carson City	*Sagebrush*	1960	8½ x 11 magazine	monthly	1,200
New Hampshire	None				
New Jersey New Jersey Reformatory, Annandale	*Annandale Highlights*	1954	8½ x 11 magazine	monthly	250
New Jersey Reformatory, Bordentown, Box 500, Bordentown	*Inside Bordentown*	1948	8½ x 14 newspaper	bi-weekly	800
New Jersey State Home for Boys, Box 500, Jamesburg	*Home Stater*	—	tabloid	monthly	500
New Jersey State Prison Farm, Lock Bag R, Rahway	The *Dome*	Nov., 1965	8½ x 11 magazine	monthly	1,200

Institution	Publication Title	Date of Founding	Type	Frequency of Publication	Circulation
New Jersey State Reformatory for Women, Clinton	*Ad Lib*	1960	8½ x 11 magazine	monthly	575
New Mexico New Mexico Boys' School, P.O. Box 38, Springer 87747	*Warriors Spear*	1955	8½ x 11 magazine	monthly	300
The Penitentiary of New Mexico, P.O. Box 1059, Santa Fe 87501	The *Enchanted News*	June, 1957	8½ x 11 magazine	bi-monthly	1,100
New York Elmira Reformatory, Elmira	The *Summary*	—	tabloid	weekly	1,200
New York Correctional Institution for Men (Rikers Island), 1500 E. 134th St., Bronx, N. Y. 10454	*Rikers Review*	1939	8½ x 11 magazine	quarterly	400
New York State Training School for Girls, Hudson 10038	*Campus Issue*	—	—	weekly	—
New York State Vocational Institution, West Coxsackie	The *Bi-Line*	Nov., 1965	pocket	bi-monthly	1,000
Otisville State Training School for Boys, Otisville 10963	*Boys Echo* [3]	1955	pocket	monthly	400
South Kortright Branch, Boys' Training Schools, Box 18, South Kortright	*Soko Tabloid*	1964	pocket	quarterly	75

INSTITUTION	PUBLICATION TITLE	DATE OF FOUND-ING	TYPE	FREQUENCY OF PUBLICA-TION	CIRCU-LATION
Western Reforma-tory for Women, Albion	*West-Al Echo*	1958	8½ x 11 magazine	quarterly	60
North Carolina Eastern Carolina Training School for Boys, Rocky Mount 27803	The *Tarheel Boy* [3]	—	8½ x 11 magazine	bi-monthly	575
Juvenile Evalua-tion Center, Swannanoa 28778	The *Center Pen*	1962	8½ x 11 magazine	monthly	150
Leonard Training School, McCain 28361	The *Leonard Comeback* [3]	Jan., 1962	8½ x 11 magazine	quarterly	400
Morrison Training School, Hoffman 28347	The *Beehive* [3]	April, 1945	8½ x 11 magazine	bi-monthly	350
Odom Prison, Rt. 1, Box 36, Jackson 27845	*Odom Hi-Rider*	Feb., 1961	pocket	bi-weekly	150
State Home & In-dustrial School for Girls (Samarcand Manor), Eagle Springs 27242	The *Pine Burr*	—	8½ x 11 magazine	quarterly	575
Stonewall Jackson Training School, Concord 28025	The *Uplift* [3]	1910	6 x 9 magazine	monthly	500
Umstead Youth Center, Box 106, Butner 27509	The *Center-prise*	1950	7 x 8½ magazine	monthly	350
North Dakota	None				
Ohio Juvenile Diag-nostic Center, 2280 W. Broad, Colum-bus 43216	*Chronicle and South Star*	—	8½ x 11 newspaper	monthly	400

Institution	Publication Title	Date of Founding	Type	Frequency of Publication	Circulation
Lebanon Correctional Institution, P.O. Box 56, Lebanon 45036	*Buccaneer*	Jan., 1961	8½ x 11 pamphlet	bi-weekly	1,700
Marion Correctional Institution, P.O. Box 57, Marion 43303	*M C Eye*	1956	pocket	monthly	1,000
Ohio Penitentiary, 254 W. Spring St., Columbus 43040	*OPNews*	April, 1892	tabloid	weekly	2,800
Ohio State Reformatory, P.O. Box 788, Mansfield 44901	The *Criterion*	Jan., 1927	tabloid	weekly	2,000
Oklahoma Oklahoma State Penitentiary, P.O. Box 97, McAlester 74501	The *Eye Opener*	—	8½ x 11 magazine	monthly	3,000
Oregon Hillcrest School of Oregon, 2450 Strong Road, Salem 97310	*Hilltop Happenings*	1925	8½ x 10	quarterly	150
MacLaren School for Boys, Rt. 1, Box 37, Woodburn 97071	The *MacLarian*	1956	tabloid	monthly	635
Oregon State Penitentiary, 2605 State St., Salem 97310	*Shadows*	1935	6¼ x 9¼ magazine	quarterly	2,100
Pennsylvania Northampton County Prison, Easton	The *Inside News*	—	8½ x 11 magazine	quarterly	—

Institution	Publication Title	Date of Founding	Type	Frequency of Publication	Circulation
State Correctional Institution at Camp Hill, Box 200, 17011	*Headliner*	1947	8 x 12 magazine	3 times a year	3,600
State Correctional Institution at Muncy, P.O. Box 180, 17756	The *Prism*	1962	8½ x 14 folded	quarterly	135
State Correctional Institution at Philadelphia, 2107 Fairmount Ave. 19130	*Eastern Echo*	1956	8¼ x 10¼ magazine	quarterly	1,050
Rhode Island Adult Correctional Institutions, P.O. Box 114, Pontiac Avenue, Howard 02834	*Hope Press*[4]	1955	8½ x 11 magazine	monthly	2,000
South Carolina Riverside School for Girls, 1925 Shivers Rd., Columbia	The *Voice*	1951	8½ x 11 magazine	quarterly	120
South Carolina Penitentiary, P.O. Box 540, Columbia 29202	*About Face*[5]	1957	tabloid	bi-weekly	1,800
South Dakota South Dakota Penitentiary, Box 911, Sioux Falls 57101	The *Messenger*	1921	pocket	quarterly	1,250
Tennessee Shelby County Penal Farm, Rt. 8, Box 500, Memphis	The *Lantern*	Jan., 1965	8½ x 7	daily	575
Tennessee State Penitentiary, Nashville, Tennessee	The *Broadcaster*	Nov., 1965	8½ x 14	bi-weekly	2,000
Youth Center, Joelton	*Four Leaf Clover*	Nov., 1965	tabloid	weekly	125

INSTITUTION	PUBLICATION TITLE	DATE OF FOUND-ING	TYPE	FREQUENCY OF PUBLICA-TION	CIRCU-LATION
Texas					
Crockett State School for Girls, P.O. Box 411, Crockett 75835	*Highlights*	—	8½ x 11 magazine	quarterly	150
Gatesville State School for Boys, P.O. Box 417, Gatesville 76528	*State School News*[3, 7]	July, 1953	tabloid	bi-weekly	2,200
Texas Department of Corrections, Box 32, Huntsville 77340	The *Echo* [6]	1924	tabloid	monthly	13,500
Utah					
Utah State Indus-trial School, 200 N. Washington Blvd., Ogden 84404	*SIS News*	Sept., 1955	8½ x 11 newspaper	monthly	300
Utah State Prison, Box 250, Draper 84020	*Pointer News*	1957	8½ x 11 magazine	quarterly	1,500
Vermont					
Vermont State Pris-on & House of Cor-rection for Men, 65 State St., Windsor 05089	*Green Moun-tain Graphic*	1955	8½ x 11 magazine	monthly	400
Women's Reforma-tory, State St., Rutland 05701	*ETC.*	1963	8½ x 11 newspaper	monthly	50
Virginia					
Bland Correctional Farm, Rt. 2, Bland 24315	The *Roller*	1956	8½ x 11 magazine	monthly	500
Janie Porter Barrett School for Girls, Hanover 23069	The *Booster*	—	8½ x 11 magazine	quarterly	150
Southhampton Farm, Capron 23829	The *Voice*	—	8½ x 11 magazine	quarterly	—

Institution	Publication Title	Date of Founding	Type	Frequency of Publication	Circulation
State Industrial Farm for Women, Goochland 23063	The *Citizen*	1941	8½ x 11 magazine	—	500
Washington Cedar Creek Forest Youth Camp, P.O. Box 38, Littlerock	*Cedar Log*	1961	8½ x 11 newspaper	quarterly	100
Green Hill School, P.O. Box 600, Chehalis 98532	The *New Leaf* [3]	1922	tabloid newspaper	monthly	1,000
Maple Lane School, Rt. 1, Box 300, Centralia 98531	*Maple Leaf*	—	8½ x 11 newspaper	monthly	—
Mission Creek Youth Forest Camp, P.O. Box 288, Belfair	*Mission Madcaps*	April, 1962	8½ x 11 newspaper	quarterly	120
Spruce Canyon Youth Forest Camp, Tiger Star Route, Coolville 99114	The *Blaze*	1961	8½ x 11 newspaper	quarterly	150
West Virginia West Virginia Forestry Camp for Boys, Davis	The *Breeze*	Oct., 1965	8½ x 11 newspaper	monthly	150
West Virginia Industrial School for Boys, Grafton	The *Cardinal*	1965	8½ x 11 newspaper	monthly	150
Wisconsin Wisconsin Correctional Institution, Fox Lake 53933	*Solar Screen*	1963	8½ x 11 magazine	monthly	700
Wisconsin School for Girls, Oregon 53575	*Campus Times*	—	—	—	—
Wisconsin State Reformatory, Green Bay 54305	The *Bay Banner*	1952	8½ x 11 newspaper	monthly	1,400

Institution	Publication Title	Date of Founding	Type	Frequency of Publication	Circulation
Wyoming					
Wyoming Industrial Institute, Box 670, Worland 82401	*Colter Review*	1963	8½ x 11 newspaper	monthly	100
Wyoming State Penitentiary, Box 407, Rawlins 82301	*Best Scene*	1962	7 x 8½ magazine	monthly	500
United States Penitentiaries					
Atlanta, Ga. 30315	The *Atlantian*	1912	8½ x 11 magazine	quarterly	4,000
Leavenworth, Kans. 66048	*New Era*	1914	8½ x 11 magazine	quarterly	3,500
Lewisburg, Pa. 17837	The *Lens*	1934	6 x 8½ magazine	monthly	2,000
McNeil Island, Wash. 98388	*Island Lantern*	1924	7 x 10 magazine	bi-monthly	1,100
Marion, Ill. 62959	*Marion Messenger*	June, 1963	8½ x 11 magazine	quarterly	750
Terre Haute, Ind. 47808	*Terrescope*	1941	8 x 10½	bi-weekly	1,000
Federal Reformatories					
Chillicothe, Ohio 45601	*Cross Roads*	1961	8½ x 11 magazine	bi-weekly	1,000
El Reno, Oklahoma 73036	*Plainstalk*	—	8½ x 11 newspaper	bi-weekly	1,000
Federal Reformatory for Women, Alderson, W. Va. 24910	The *Eagle*	Nov., 1933	8 x 10½ magazine	quarterly	750
Lompoc, California 93438	*Narrator*	1965	8½ x 14	weekly	1,100
Petersburg, Virginia 23804	The *Petersburg Bulletin*	1952	8½ x 11 magazine	quarterly	25

INSTITUTION	PUBLICATION TITLE	DATE OF FOUNDING	TYPE	FREQUENCY OF PUBLICATION	CIRCULATION
Institutions for Juvenile and Youth Offenders					
Federal Correctional Institution, Ashland, Kentucky 41101	*Barometer*	1940	8½ x 11 newspaper	bi-weekly	500
Federal Correctional Institution, Englewood, Colo. 80110	The *Chinook*	1962	8 x 10½ newspaper	weekly	200
Federal Youth Camp, Tucson, Arizona 85703	*Hilltopper*	1957	8½ x 11 magazine	weekly	150
National Training School for Boys, Washington, D. C. 20013	*NTS Progress*	1953	8½ x 11 newsmagazine	bi-weekly	—
Federal Correctional Institutions					
Danbury, Conn. 06813	*Dan Muse*	1950	8½ x 11 magazine	quarterly	700
Milan, Mich. 48160	The *Insider*	Aug., 1965	8½ x 11 magazine	monthly	550
Sandstone, Minn. 55072	*Northernaire*	1962	pocket	quarterly	450
Seagoville, Texas 75159	*Seagozette*	late 1940's	8½ x 11 magazine	quarterly	700
Terminal Island, Los Angeles, California 90731	*T.I. News*	1955	8½ x 11 magazine	monthly	450
Texarkana, Texas 75502	The *Crossroads*	—	8½ x 11 magazine	quarterly	700
Federal Prison Camps					
Eglin Air Force Base, Florida 32542	*Eglin Chronicle*	1963	8½ x 11 magazine	monthly	250
Federal Medical Center					
Medical Center for Federal Prisoners, Springfield, Mo. 65802	The *Epitome*	May, 1966	pocket magazine	monthly	500

INSTITUTION	PUBLICATION TITLE	DATE OF FOUND-ING	TYPE	FREQUENCY OF PUBLICA-TION	CIRCU-LATION
Department of the Army					
U. S. Disciplinary Barracks, Ft. Leav-enworth, Kansas 66027	*Stray Shots*	—	8½ x 11 magazine	monthly	800

1. Also covers State Cattle Ranch at Greensboro.

2. San Quentin is a good example of the institutions in which specialized publications augment the general periodical. In addition to the *San Quentin News,* there is an Alcoholics Anonymous Newsletter, a high school paper, a Holy Name Society Newsletter, and a Chess Club Newsletter.

3. Staff produced; students contribute material and/or do print shop work.

4. Serves the five adult institutions of Rhode Island.

5. Serves the other six state correctional institutions as well as the penitentiary.

6. Serves all fourteen state adult institutions.

7. Six other schools included in its coverage.

APPENDIX B
An Explanation of Methodology and a Summary of Results

METHODOLOGY

The main source of data for this study was a questionnaire mailed to all state and federal correctional institutions in the United States (with the exception of mental hospitals, military institutions, short-term diagnostic centers, and branch institutions) as listed in the August, 1965, *Directory of State and Federal Correctional Institutions* published by the American Correctional Association.

Additional questionnaires were sent to a few county and military institutions whose publishing activities were first reported by a respondent on the original list. Responses were received from 413 out of 452 institutions (91.3 per cent).

Information of a more detailed nature was obtained through depth interviews with convicts and publication supervisors at the Ohio, Maryland, and Southern Illinois state penitentiaries; the Indiana Reformatory; the Alderson, West Virginia, Federal Reformatory for Women; and the Terre Haute, Indiana, United States Penitentiary.

To evaluate the content of prison publications, a qualitative analysis of available publications was made. Copies of contemporary issues were sought during a three and one-half year period—January, 1963, to June, 1966—and copies of 162 publications were obtained. The file for each publication ranged from one copy to a complete set of issues for more than three years. All copies were carefully studied, and this examination provided the basis for many qualitative judgments. As a check on these judgments, a structured content analysis was performed on a sample using the available publications of the basic prison of each state, plus the federal penitentiaries. Table 1 (p. 202) shows the results of this analysis.

SUMMARY OF RESULTS

Objective Responses
Total number of penal publications: 222

Total institutions covered by penal publications: 253
Total penal press circulation: 240,036
Circulation to outside readers: 80,416
Frequency of publication:

Daily	1
Weekly	21
Bi-weekly	31
Monthly	96
Bi-monthly	18
Quarterly	48
Thrice yearly	1
Twice yearly	1
Irregular	3
Unreported	2

Format:

Magazine	108
Newspaper	81
Combination	33

Most popular sizes:

8½ x 11	120
tabloid newspaper	35
pocket magazine	12

Printing Process:

Mimeograph	99
Letterpress	49
Offset	38
Spirit duplicating	18
Combinations	18

    Mimeograph and offset, 1; mimeograph and silk screen, 6; mimeograph and letterpress, 1; letterpress and silk screen, 2; letterpress and offset, 5; offset and silk screen, 3.

Administrators who supervise the publication:

Supervisor of Education	96
Instructors or others from education department	76
Associate Warden, Treatment	28
Outside journalist	4

Warden	2 (19 others reported warden's ultimate responsibility)
Other	14
No response	2

Subscription practices:

No charge	173
Nominal charge ($1 to $2 per year)	36
No response	13

Specialized publications:

Alcoholics Anonymous	79
Other (Drugs Anonymous, Synanon, JayCees, Holy Name Society, Chess Club, Checks Anonymous, etc.)	34

EVALUATIVE RESPONSES

Do you think publications work has any special rehabilitative effect for the inmates who have major staff positions on the publications?

Yes	172
No	20
No answer	30

Have there been any special instances in which the publication has been an administrative problem?

Yes	44
No	158
No answer	20

Have you had to discontinue publication or reclassify editors for disciplinary reasons connected with the publication?

Yes	20
No	176
No answer	26

Have there been any instances in which the publication has been a special help for the administration?

Yes	149
No	49
No answer	24

DISTRIBUTION OF SPACE (BY PERCENTAGE OF TOTAL
SPACE) DEVOTED TO VARIOUS TYPES OF CONTENT
BY 56 SELECTED PRISON PUBLICATIONS *
(In Numbers of Publications)

PERCENT-AGE OF TOTAL SPACE USED	FICTION	POETRY	OFFICIAL AN-NOUNCE-MENTS	GEN-ERAL NEWS	HUMOR	RE-PRINTS
None	31	17	23		2	18
1–5	8	33	25		33	15
6–10	8	6	3		15	14
11–15	4		2		3	3
16–20	2		3		1	4
21–25	1				2	2
26–30	2			1		
31–35				1	٭	
36–40				1		
41–50				3		
51–60				7		
61–70				8		
71–80				18		
81–90				13		
91–100				4		

* Available publications from the basic prison of each state plus the federal
penitentiaries were used. Of the 68 institutions originally selected for
participation in this study, 62 (91 per cent) were producing publications.
A minimum of four copies was provided for analysis by 56 (90 per cent)
of these institutions. Square inches of printed area were used to determine
the percentages; percentages were rounded off at the lowest whole number.

INDEX